The Art of After-Sales Marketing

Vladislav Dobrokhotov

Published by Vladislav Dobrokhotov, 2023.

THE ART OF AFTER-SALES MARKETING

First edition. August 7, 2023.

Copyright © 2023 Vladislav Dobrokhotov.

ISBN: 979-8223706250

Written by Vladislav Dobrokhotov.

Table of Contents

Foreword by Dr Trevor Brignall

THIS BOOK IS WRITTEN in an easily digestible format that walks the reader through a journey of exploration on a key area of marketing that adds significant value to the profitability of any organisation, large or small. Customer acquisition and, importantly, retention are essential not only to commercial operations but also not-for-profit and membership organisations.

The book will appeal to a wide range of readers, ranging from those on a journey of discovery wishing to learn more about this important topic to the seasoned practitioner seeking a useful checklist.

For centuries, the most powerful stories and impacts have been delivered not through words but pictures and music -from the paintings of prehistoric cavemen to the work of Andy Warhol, the compositions of Mozart to those of Bob Dylan and Paul McCartney. The old adage, a picture paints a thousand words, enables marketers to quickly translate concepts and ideas into images. Using art and artists, the author illustrates how companies infuse their brands with character, individuality, and emotion.

Dr Trevor Brignall

Prologue: The Artist and the Emperor

ONCE UPON A TIME, AN emperor asked an artist to paint the Himalayas on the walls of his palace. The artist, a Zen master, said he would need to live in the Himalayas for three years to do so. The emperor asked:

-"Will it take you three years?"

The artist replied:

-"I ask for the minimum time because I cannot paint them until I become a part of the Himalayas. I need to go there and dissolve in them."

Three years passed, and the artist returned. He painted the wall in three days. The emperor came to see. It was a wonder! He had never seen such beautiful mountains. Even the real Himalayas seemed pale in comparison. He stood for a long time, admiring, and then noticed:

-"I see a path here. Where does it lead?"

The artist answered:

-"We can go and see."

And they left, never to return.

Introduction

In essence, after-sales marketing is the finishing touch on your brand's masterpiece, the detail that can turn a satisfied customer into a loyal brand advocate.

MUCH LIKE AN ARTIST'S canvas, the world of marketing is full of endless possibilities and vibrant colors, each hue representing a different approach to connecting with customers. One of this palette's most understated yet potent colors is the art of after-sales.

Just as an artist breathes life into a blank canvas, marketers infuse brands with character, individuality, and emotion. The parallels between marketers and artists are numerous. Both see the world through a unique lens, carefully curating experiences and narratives that evoke emotion and forge connections.

Artists don't merely create a piece of art; they tell a story through it. Similarly, a marketer doesn't just sell a product or service; they narrate the brand's story, values, vision, and the problems it solves.

However, the most compelling stories don't conclude at the point of sale. Much like a captivating novel or a gripping movie, they leave the audience yearning for more. This is where after-sales marketing enters the narrative. It's the epilogue that keeps the customer engaged, extending the relationship beyond the initial transaction and forging a lasting bond between the brand and its customers.

After-sales marketing is an art that requires finesse and creativity. When mastered, it serves as a powerful tool to nurture customer relationships, enhance brand loyalty, and increase customer lifetime value.

Embracing this mindset requires seeing after-sales not merely as a post-purchase obligation but as an opportunity for ongoing storytelling and relationship-building. This perspective empowers marketers to design creative, engaging, memorable experiences that resonate deeply with customers.

In this book, we will delve deeper into the canvas of possibilities, exploring the vast array of after-sales strategies and techniques available to marketers. We'll learn how to wield the brush with precision, selecting the right hues to paint a captivating picture that resonates with our audience, turning satisfied customers into loyal brand advocates.

Chapter 1: The Artist's Perspective

———

IN THE MARKETING REALM, we often find ourselves veering into a world that transcends pure business transactions. From the lens of an artist, marketing is an opportunity to express our brand's narrative, values, vision, and solutions, painting a vivid canvas that profoundly resonates with our audience.

In this opening chapter, we aim to uncover how an artistic perspective can elevate your after-sales marketing strategy and customer relationships and explore the parallels between the creators of art and architects of marketing campaigns. We will emphasize the integral role of after-sales communications in our creative endeavor, often serving as the final, unforgettable stroke of our brand's masterpiece.

Crafting a Compelling Brand Story

At the heart of every successful brand lies a compelling story, a narrative that integrates the facts about your products or services with the emotions and associations they spark in customers' minds.

Take Patagonia, for example, the outdoor clothing and gear brand. Patagonia's story isn't solely about selling high-quality outdoor gear. It's a narrative about environmental sustainability and the spirit of adventure, consistently conveyed across all customer touchpoints. The brand connects deeply with customers who align with these values.

Now, pause for a moment to reflect on your brand's story. Does it evoke specific emotions or associations?

Living the Brand Values

Values serve as the backbone of a brand, the beliefs that guide its actions, unify its employees, and differentiate it from its competitors. These principles help define how a brand operates in its industry and marketplace.

Consider Google, a brand that centers around a core value - the user. Google's user-focused operations extend from its intuitive search engine design to its highly responsive customer support. This user-centric value, integral to Google's brand story, significantly contributes to its success in the competitive tech industry.

Think about your brand's values. Are they clearly communicated and demonstrated through your actions?

Embracing the Brand Vision

A brand's vision is a long-term goal or aspiration, providing a roadmap for strategic planning and decision-making.

Tesla perfectly illustrates their vision statement "to create the most compelling car company of the 21st century by driving the world's transition to electric vehicles." This bold vision not only inspires Tesla's employees and customers but also distinctly sets it apart in the crowded automotive market.

What is your brand's vision? Does it inspire and differentiate your brand from its competitors?

Problem-Solving: The Heart of Business

At its core, every business exists to solve a problem or meet its customers' needs. By clearly communicating the problems your brand solves, you can connect more profoundly with your customers and differentiate your brand from competitors.

Airbnb, for example, doesn't just provide a platform for accommodation; it strives to make people feel at home anywhere in the world. This solution-focused approach is an essential part of Airbnb's brand narrative, significantly contributing to its global success.

What problems does your brand solve? How do you communicate these solutions to your customers?

The Art of After-Sales Marketing in Storytelling

After-sales experience is a critical stage in the customer journey and an ideal platform to reinforce your brand's story, values, vision, and problem-solving capabilities. It's your chance to follow through on your promises and demonstrate your brand's commitment to customer satisfaction. This finishing touch on your brand masterpiece is the detail that can transform a satisfied customer into a devoted brand advocate.

As we navigate the art of after-sales, remember this artist's perspective. Every interaction is a unique opportunity to add depth and detail to our masterpiece to strengthen our brand narrative.

The Harmonious Perspective of Marketers and Artists

The worlds of marketing and artistry may seem distinct. However, on closer examination, we discover a shared perspective. Both marketers and artists are storytellers, weaving narratives that emotionally engage and motivate their audience. They need a clear vision to guide their creations and strategies. Both professions focus on creating value and know that attention to detail significantly contributes to their overall work impact.

With an artist's mindset, marketers can enhance their approach, crafting brand experiences that satisfy, inspire, and move customers.

Drawing Parallels: Artists and Marketers

To further emphasize the connection between marketing and art, let's consider a metaphorical comparison between notable artists and their marketing counterparts:

Pablo Picasso - Branding Expert

Picasso, celebrated for his innovative and adaptable style, mirrors the qualities of a branding expert. Picasso's ability to reinvent his style could be likened to the dynamic nature of crafting compelling and innovative brand identities.

Ludwig van Beethoven - Content Marketer

Beethoven's passionate and groundbreaking compositions echo the role of a content marketer. They craft content that emotionally resonates with audiences, breaking conventions to create truly engaging and memorable experiences.

Steven Spielberg - Video Marketing Specialist

Spielberg, a master storyteller, could be seen as a video marketing specialist. His ability to weave intricate narratives and evoke deep emotional responses mirrors the craft of creating compelling video content that tells a brand's story.

Maya Angelou - Social Media Manager

With her empathetic communication style and ability to connect with diverse audiences, Angelou mirrors a social media manager's role. Her skills could translate into cultivating strong online communities, fostering meaningful conversations, and a sense of belonging.

Frank Lloyd Wright - User Experience (UX) Designer

Wright's architectural designs, harmonious with their surroundings and tailored to the needs of their inhabitants, embody the principles of a UX designer. This role involves creating digital interfaces that are aesthetically pleasing but also intuitive, responsive, and user-friendly.

These examples highlight the intersection of art and marketing, emphasizing the principles of creativity, innovation, and emotional resonance in both spheres. By adopting an artist's mindset, marketers can craft campaigns that are effective but also engaging, memorable, and deeply resonant with their audience.

Practical Applications: Turning Artistic After-Sales Marketing into Reality

As we continue to interpret the concept of viewing after-sales marketing from an artist's perspective, we must also understand how to apply this mindset practically in our businesses. Here are several actionable approaches to do so:

Develop Your Brand Story Canvas:

Just as an artist needs a canvas to start painting, marketers need a structure to craft their brand story. Start by clearly defining the critical elements of your brand story: who you are, what you do, why you do it, and how you're different from your competitors. Use these elements as your canvas to develop a cohesive and compelling brand narrative.

Express Your Brand Values in After-Sales Service:

Think about how your brand values can manifest themselves in your after-sales service. For instance, if one of your core values is 'transparency,' this could mean providing clear, comprehensive information about product care, warranty details, and the return policy. If 'empathy' is a crucial value, it could translate into personalized after-sales communication or swift resolution of customer issues.

Elevate Your Brand Vision Through After-Sales:

Your brand vision is an aspirational goal that you aim to achieve. Explore how your after-sales service can contribute to realizing this vision. For example, if your vision involves sustainability, you might incorporate eco-friendly packaging or carbon-neutral delivery in your after-sales processes.

Identify and Solve Problems Through After-Sales:

Pay close attention to customer feedback and complaints in the after-sales phase. These can provide valuable insights into the problems customers face, enabling you to find solutions and improve your products or services. For instance, if customers frequently struggle with product setup, you could address this by providing detailed instruction manuals or video guides.

Channel Renowned Artists for Inspiration:

Drawing from the analogies between renowned artists and marketing specializations, consider how you might channel the creativity and ingenuity of these artists in your after-sales marketing.

Like Picasso, constantly seek to innovate and adapt your after-sales strategies. Be a Beethoven in content creation for after-sales communication. Emulate Spielberg's storytelling prowess to captivate your customers even after their purchase. Use Angelou's empathetic communication style to foster strong relationships with customers. And finally, channel Wright's user-centric design approach to ensure your after-sales processes are tailored to your customers' needs.

By applying these strategies, you can start to view and shape your after-sales marketing with an artist's eye, creating a masterpiece that satisfies your customers and turns them into loyal advocates for your brand. This approach to after-sales marketing, underpinned by creativity and emotional resonance, is both an art and a science - a balance that, when struck, can lead to remarkable results.

Chapter 2: Crafting the Masterpiece: An Exploration of After-Sales Marketing

THE ACT OF SELLING is only the first stroke on the canvas of customer experience; after-sales marketing is the spectrum of colors that fill the rest of the painting, transforming it from a simple transaction into an enduring relationship. Let's explore it further to understand its intricacies and transformational role in the customer journey.

Comparing Key Marketing Activities: Acquisition, Retention, and Advocacy

Understanding the different facets of marketing is crucial for any business looking to thrive in today's competitive landscape. Each element - acquiring new customers, increasing retention, and turning customers into brand advocates - plays a significant role in the overall marketing strategy.

However, the goals, activities, metrics, benefits, and challenges associated with each can vary widely. The following table provides a comparison of these three crucial marketing activities to shed light on their unique characteristics and interconnections:

Comparing Key Marketing Activities: Acquisition, Retention, and Advocacy

	Acquiring New Customers	**Increasing Retention**	**Turning Customers into Brand Advocates**
Goals	Raise awareness; Generate interest; Convert interest into sales	Build customer loyalty; Encourage repeat purchases; Improve customer satisfaction	Amplify brand message; Leverage word-of-mouth marketing; Build a community around the brand
Key Activities	Content marketing; Paid advertising; SEO; Social media marketing; Email marketing	After-sales service; Loyalty programs; Personalized offers; Customer feedback and improvement	Referral programs; User-generated content; Brand ambassador programs; Excellent customer service; Community events
Key Metrics	Customer acquisition cost (CAC); Conversion rate; Number of leads	Customer retention rate; Customer churn rate; Customer lifetime value (CLV)	Net Promoter Score (NPS); Number of referrals; Social media shares/engagement
Benefits	Expands customer base; Increases market share; Fuels business growth	Reduces costs (since it's more expensive to acquire new customers than to keep existing ones); Provides a steady revenue stream	Generates free advertising; Enhances brand reputation; Builds trust with prospective customers
Challenges	Can be costly; Requires constant optimization to reach the right audience	Requires ongoing engagement and excellent customer service; Customers' needs and expectations may evolve over time	Not all customers will become advocates; Requires consistent, positive brand experiences

The Unfolding Tale of Acquisition, Retention, and Advocacy: Eco Essentials

Let us now embark on a captivating journey that brings the concepts of acquisition, retention, and advocacy to life. Through the compelling narrative of Eco Essentials, a budding online store in the bustling city of Bizville, we'll uncover the transformative power of effective post-purchase marketing strategies. This real-world illustration presents the application of the theoretical concepts discussed so far in a relatable, easy-to-grasp manner.

As we traverse through the stages of customer acquisition, nurturing a relationship, and fostering brand advocacy, we'll realize the importance of each phase in crafting an enduring and fruitful customer-brand relationship. So, get ready to dive into the fascinating story of Eco Essentials and its passionate customer, Jake.

Once upon a time, in the bustling city of Bizville, lived a young entrepreneur named Emma. Emma recently launched her "Eco Essentials" online store, which sells eco-friendly products.

Acquisition: The First Meeting

Jake stumbled upon Eco Essentials through a cleverly crafted social media campaign promoting sustainable living. Intrigued, he visited the website and was instantly impressed by the array of eco-friendly products.

What caught his eye was the store's commitment to sustainability, not just in products but also in packaging and shipping methods. The digital marketing campaign, coupled with the store's ethos, successfully acquired Jake as a new customer.

Retention: The Nurturing Relationship

Jake's relationship with Eco Essentials continued after his first purchase. Emma ensured that Jake was cared for even after the sales transaction. He received a personalized thank you email guiding him on making the most of his new eco-friendly products.

He was also subscribed to a monthly newsletter providing tips on sustainable living, updates on new products, and exclusive discounts. This customer nurturing strategy made Jake feel valued and kept him engaged, increasing his loyalty to Eco Essentials.

Advocacy: Becoming a Brand Advocate

One day, Jake received an unexpected package from Eco Essentials. It was a complimentary eco-friendly product, accompanied by a note of appreciation for his continued support for the brand and the cause of sustainability. Jake was touched by this unexpected gesture of goodwill.

This was more than just a business transaction for him - it was a relationship based on shared values. Emma's commitment to enhancing customer experience retained Jake as a customer and transformed him into a passionate brand advocate.

Word of mouth, they say, is the best form of advertising, and this rang true for Eco Essentials. Jake shared his positive experiences with friends, family, and social media followers. His authentic, personal endorsement of Eco Essentials brought in more customers who shared the same passion for sustainability.

This narrative encapsulates the journey from acquisition to advocacy, highlighting the pivotal role of effective after-sales marketing strategies in transforming customers into brand advocates.

The Luminary Evolution of After-Sales Marketing

THE ART OF AFTER-SALES MARKETING

This concept is not new; it has been part of the business lexicon for decades. However, it was traditionally sidelined as a minor appendage to the sales process, with businesses' primary focus being acquiring new customers.

Early after-sales efforts were limited to simple gestures such as sending thank-you notes, providing warranties, or offering routine maintenance services. But as competition increased and the cost of acquiring new customers continued to rise, businesses began to realize the importance of nurturing existing customers.

Fast forward to today, and after-sales marketing has undergone a massive transformation. It's no longer just satisfying the customer; it's about exceeding their expectations, surprising them with value at every step, and building an enduring relationship that turns one-time buyers into loyal customers and brand advocates. In the digital age, the scope of after-sales marketing has broadened exponentially, powered by technology and data-driven insights.

Personalized email marketing, loyalty programs, AI-driven product recommendations, comprehensive customer service, and interactive content - the tools at our disposal have grown, and so have the opportunities for creating memorable customer experiences.

Influence on Customer Perception: Casting a Positive Spell

Customer journey mapping has revealed an important truth: the post-purchase experience is as critical, if not more so, than the buying process. After-sales marketing is the invisible choreographer directing this dance, guiding the customer through different touchpoints and ensuring the experience is seamless, consistent, and valuable.

Every interaction a customer has with your brand contributes to their perception of you. A well-executed after-sales strategy doesn't just prevent buyer's remorse; it affirms the customer's purchase decision, making them feel confident and happy about choosing your brand.

But it's not just about affirmation; it's also about enrichment. Offering valuable content related to the purchased product or service, providing tips on usage, giving updates on new features, or simply sharing relevant industry news are ways to add value to the customer's life, enhancing their perception of your brand.

And then there's the element of surprise. Nothing leaves a lasting positive impression like a pleasant surprise. An unexpected discount on the next purchase, a complimentary upgrade, or a small token of appreciation can enchant your customers and cast a favorable spell on their perception.

Seizing the Overlooked Opportunity: Harnessing the Power of After-Sales Marketing

After-sales marketing is like the final act in a thrilling play - a strategic, well-crafted closure that leaves audiences feeling valued and eager to return for the next show. Yet, surprisingly, many businesses lower the curtain too soon, neglecting this critical stage of the customer journey. This tendency to overlook after-sales marketing leaves a significant gap that savvy businesses can exploit to stand out from the crowd.

Let's examine the comparative impact of implementing robust after-sales marketing strategies versus the conventional transaction-focused approach. The following table sheds light on this aspect, highlighting the stark differences and potential benefits reaped by businesses that make after-sales marketing an integral part of their overall strategy:

THE ART OF AFTER-SALES MARKETING

ASM-Driven vs Transaction-Focused Companies

	ASM-Driven Companies	Transaction-focused Companies
Customer Loyalty	High, as continuous engagement and value addition help retain customers and drive repeat purchases.	Low, due to limited post-purchase engagement and a transactional approach.
Customer Lifetime Value	High, as the focus is on nurturing long-term relationships with customers, which leads to repeat business.	Limited, as the emphasis is primarily on acquiring new customers rather than retaining existing ones.
Brand Advocacy	Strong, as satisfied customers become brand ambassadors, driving word-of-mouth marketing and referrals.	Weak, due to a lack of sufficient positive customer experiences to encourage advocacy.
Competitive Advantage	Significant, as after-sales service can be a key differentiator in markets where product offerings are similar.	Limited, as lack of effective after-sales service can make a company's offering undifferentiated.
Cost Efficiency	More cost-effective in the long run, as retaining customers is generally more economical than acquiring new ones.	More costly, as companies without a strong after-sales marketing strategy tend to rely on costlier customer acquisition strategies.
Customer Feedback & Continuous Improvement	Regular, as strong after-sales engagement provides opportunities to solicit customer feedback and make continuous improvements.	Sporadic or non-existent, leading to missed opportunities for improvement and innovation.

By adopting a robust after-sales marketing strategy, companies can build lasting customer relationships, boost customer loyalty and lifetime value, differentiate themselves from competitors, and drive continuous improvement and innovation. This can lead to increased profitability and foster a more customer-centric organizational culture.

A Deep Dive into After-Sales Marketing Techniques

While we've mentioned a few after-sales marketing techniques like personalized email campaigns, loyalty programs, and customer feedback systems, there's much more to be explored. How do these techniques work? How can they be implemented effectively? How do they contribute to the customer experience and perception? What are some of the best practices and common pitfalls to avoid? And most importantly, how have they been used successfully by businesses worldwide?

We'll answer all these questions and more in the following chapters, where we'll take a detailed look at each technique. We'll also share real-world examples of successful after-sales strategies, providing practical insights and actionable tips you can apply to your business.

With this chapter, we've only begun to scrape the surface of after-sales marketing. As we progress, we'll dive deeper, exploring the nuances of after-sales strategies and uncovering the secrets to creating an unforgettable customer journey. Stay tuned as we continue our exploration, unveiling the colors that will help you create your masterpiece of customer experience.

Chapter 3: The Cornerstones of After-Sales Marketing

IN THIS PIVOTAL CHAPTER, we dive into the essence of after-sales marketing - Customer Retention and Brand Advocacy. These twin pillars are instrumental in sculpting a resilient and dynamic marketing strategy that engenders a cyclical process of turning satisfied customers into passionate brand advocates.

Becoming proficient in these foundational aspects can remarkably enhance customer relations, embedding a lasting impression of your brand within the consumer psyche.

This journey involves holding on to your customer base and inspiring them to become active promoters of your brand, fostering organic growth, and solidifying your business reputation.

Customer Retention: Crafting a Solid Foundation

Retaining existing customers is not merely a cost-effective strategy compared to acquiring new ones; it also guarantees a consistent stream of revenue, positive reviews, and invaluable word-of-mouth referrals.

An article from Harvard Business Review[1] emphasizes the cost-effectiveness of customer retention over customer acquisition. It indicates that acquiring a new customer is anywhere from five to 25 times more expensive than retaining an existing one.

The high cost of customer acquisition compared to customer retention can be attributed to several factors:

---

1. https://hbr.org/2014/10/the-value-of-keeping-the-right-customers

Marketing Costs:

Acquiring new customers typically involves higher marketing and advertising expenses. Businesses need to make potential customers aware of their products or services and convince them of their value. This often requires considerable effort and expense in marketing campaigns, including online advertising, print media, television ads, and more.

Sales and Promotions:

To entice new customers, businesses often offer special deals, discounts, or promotional offers. While these can be effective in attracting new customers, they also reduce the initial revenue from those customers.

Onboarding Costs:

New customers may require assistance learning to navigate and use a company's products or services. This could involve customer service calls, user manuals, training, and more. All of these require resources and thus represent a cost.

Uncertainty:

With new customers, there's always an element of uncertainty. Even after you've incurred the cost to acquire them, there's no guarantee they will stick around. On the other hand, existing customers have already demonstrated a willingness to purchase your product or service.

Profitability:

Existing customers can often be more profitable. They may be more likely to purchase other products or services, upgrade their current membership level, or make repeat purchases. They're also more likely to refer others to your business, providing free advertising.

THE ART OF AFTER-SALES MARKETING

As we transition from the broader landscape of customer retention, a concept emerges that is inextricably linked to it — the Customer Lifetime Value (CLV). A successful retention strategy sets the stage for this critical metric, quantifying the total net profit a company expects to earn from a single customer. Understanding and accurately calculating CLV empowers businesses to make informed decisions about resource allocation between retaining existing customers and acquiring new ones.

Understanding Customer Lifetime Value

The CLV is a measure of the net profit a business anticipates gaining over the entirety of its relationship with a customer. It factors in the costs involved in customer acquisition and the revenue earned throughout the relationship.

As a general guideline, the lifetime value should ideally be three times more than the cost of customer acquisition. This calculation empowers businesses to view their customers not merely as individual transactions but as long-term, valuable assets.

In online retail, for example, subscribers to premium services tend to have a higher lifetime value, often more than double compared to regular customers.

Understanding these differences is crucial in optimizing customer acquisition and retention strategies which can dramatically alter your perspective, thus influencing marketing and sales strategies.

Unveiling Buyer's Remorse and Post-Purchase Dissonance

The psychological aspect of purchasing plays a crucial role in customer retention. Buyers often experience post-purchase dissonance or buyer's remorse after a transaction. This is particularly prevalent in e-commerce, where customers can't see, touch, or try an item before buying it.

This sense of remorse centers on more significant purchases, such as homes and cars. In contrast, post-purchase dissonance often results from purchasing less expensive items like food and clothing. Thus, managing such emotions is integral to after-sales customer service and communication.

This is the stage at which your business should strive to maintain customer interest and commitment, transforming one-time shoppers into loyal patrons. To accomplish this, we must comprehend what our customers desire after a purchase, devise strategies to fulfill these needs, measure the influence of our efforts, and perpetually learn and adapt.

Understanding Customer Psychology Post-Purchase

When a customer completes a purchase, their mindset shifts from anticipation to assessment. They begin to seek validation for their decision, hoping the product or service delivers as advertised and satisfies their requirements. This stage offers a golden opportunity for businesses to foster enduring relationships and cultivate customer loyalty.

Let's look into what customers typically expect post-purchase and consider a few examples of how businesses across different industries are meeting these expectations:

Validation and Satisfaction:

The post-purchase phase is where customers affirm their buying decisions. This is a critical moment for brands to ensure that the product or service delivers on its promises and satisfies customer needs. Companies that maintain high-quality standards in their products or services gain a significant edge. For instance, Apple Inc. is reputed for its superior quality and design, consistently impressing its customer base, thereby ensuring customer retention.

Trust and Support:

Post-purchase, customers also look for reliable and accessible customer support. The promptness and effectiveness of issue resolution heavily influence customer perception and trust in the brand. Businesses like Zappos have set benchmarks in this domain by offering round-the-clock support and going the extra mile to reassure customers even after their purchase.

Learning and Guidance:

Customers value post-purchase guidance and education on using and benefiting from their investment optimally, particularly for complex products. This is where comprehensive guides, tutorials, and support from the brand can enhance the overall customer experience. Software companies often excel in this area, providing extensive knowledge bases, online tutorials, and webinars.

Incorporating these post-purchase needs into your business strategy can significantly enhance customer satisfaction and establish enduring relationships, transforming your customers into repeat buyers and advocates for your brand.

Designing Customer Retention Strategies

Creating a compelling customer retention strategy requires deliberate planning, execution, and analysis. This ongoing process necessitates a deep understanding of your customers and a commitment to providing value at every stage of their journey. Let's add an artistic touch to the customer retention strategy:

Develop a Deep Empathy for Your Customers:

Much like an artist fully immerses themselves in their subject, you should strive to understand your customers deeply, including their motivations, fears, aspirations, and lifestyle. This empathetic approach will inform more meaningful engagement strategies.

Craft a Unique Brand Narrative:

Artists narrate stories through their creations, and your brand should emulate this. Develop a distinctive narrative aligned with your brand's values, and ensure this story resonates with your customers' beliefs and aspirations. Integrate this narrative into all your after-sales marketing efforts.

Design a Masterful Customer Experience:

Artists invoke emotions through their work, and your customer experience should aim to achieve the same. Deliberately design each customer interaction to evoke positive emotions, create a memorable experience, and foster loyalty.

Continued Engagement:

The interaction between a brand and a customer should not end once a purchase is made. Proactive communication, like a follow-up email or a check-in call, reassures customers of their value to the business. Chewy is renowned for sending personalized, handwritten thank-you notes to their customers, expressing genuine care for their pets and gratitude for their business.

Personalization:

Tailoring post-purchase interactions to individual customers not only meets their specific needs but also makes them feel unique and valued. A great example of this approach is Amazon's recommendation system. By suggesting products based on customers' purchases and browsing history, Amazon creates a more personalized and convenient shopping experience.

This process, akin to painting a masterpiece, requires patience, dedication, and the understanding that it's a continuous journey of improvement.

Expanding the Role of Technology in Customer Retention

In today's fast-paced, technologically-driven world, businesses can harness the power of AI and machine learning to supercharge their customer retention strategies.

For instance, customer relationship management (CRM) platforms use AI to analyze customer behavior and preferences, enabling businesses to predict future buying habits and tailor offers accordingly. AI-powered chatbots provide round-the-clock customer service, efficiently handling inquiries and resolving issues.

Netflix offers another compelling example. It employs advanced machine learning algorithms to analyze viewing habits and deliver personalized content recommendations, a strategy that has significantly contributed to its high customer retention rate.

These examples represent just a glimpse of the transformative power of technology in customer retention. As you strategize for your business, ask yourself: How can your business leverage technology to better understand, engage, and retain customers?

Reflective Pause: Examining Your Retention Practices

At this juncture, let's take a moment to reflect on your own business. What steps are you taking to understand your customers' post-purchase mindset? Which of the retention strategies discussed above can you begin to implement? How could AI or machine learning contribute to your retention efforts?

An ongoing, robust customer retention strategy is essential for businesses to thrive in today's competitive landscape. By treating customer retention as an art, your business can foster deep connections, ensuring customer loyalty and long-term success.

Brand Advocacy: Turning Customers into Your Marketing Knights

Brand advocacy is another holy grail of after-sales marketing. It is when customers become so enchanted with your brand that they voluntarily become your advocates, spreading the word about it within their networks. They're not just repeat buyers; they're brand promoters who drive word-of-mouth marketing, one of the most influential and credible forms of marketing.

Creating brand advocates is not a chance occurrence; it results from a well-planned, meticulously executed strategy. This strategy should be centered around exceeding customer expectations consistently, surprising them with value, and building an emotional connection that transcends the functional benefits of the product or service.

Just as an engaging piece of art can captivate its audience, prompting whispers of awe and admiration, so too can a well-executed brand advocacy strategy inspire customers to share their positive experiences with your brand. In this section, we dive deep into the artistry of brand advocacy, exploring its psychological underpinnings and the ethical considerations to remember while deploying it.

The Masterstroke: Turning Customers into Brand Advocates

The real masterpiece of a customer-centric brand is a satisfied customer transformed into a zealous advocate. These advocates are customers so captivated by their experience with your brand that they voluntarily become storytellers within their circles. A Nielsen study[2] emphasizes the potency of such narratives, highlighting that 92% of consumers trust recommendations from friends and family more than traditional advertising.

Delving Deeper into the Canvas: The Psychology of Word-of-Mouth

Like an artist recognizing the subtle nuances of color and texture to evoke a particular emotion, a successful marketer understands the psychological principles that power word-of-mouth marketing.

Two standout principles are social proof and trust, which are more than just theoretical constructs; they're deeply rooted in human behavior. Understanding them is crucial to fostering brand advocacy successfully.

Social Proof

The principle of social proof is derived from the psychological phenomenon where people mirror the actions and behaviors of others, especially in ambiguous or unfamiliar situations. They trust the crowd's judgment, viewing it as 'proof' of the correct or preferred behavior.

In after-sales marketing, social proof can be leveraged in various ways, including displaying customer testimonials, showcasing user-generated content, or highlighting popularity metrics (like 'best-seller' tags or 'X people bought this').

For instance, when potential customers see others praising a product or service, their confidence in the offering increases. They feel reassured about their decision to engage with a product or service, enhancing their likelihood to purchase, repurchase, and recommend. Social proof

---

2. https://www.nielsen.com/insights/2012/consumer-trust-in-online-social-and-mobile-
   advertising-grows/

thus plays a significant role in building trust and converting customers into brand advocates.

Trust

Trust, the second principle, is foundational in any relationship between customers and brands. It is the belief or confidence that the other party will act in one's best interest. In after-sales marketing, trust is built when businesses consistently meet or exceed customer expectations, deliver on their promises, and demonstrate transparency and honesty in their interactions.

Customers who trust a brand feel more secure in investing in its offerings, knowing they won't be deceived or let down. This security prompts them to continue their patronage and recommend the brand to others, thereby acting as brand advocates.

For example, a customer who trusts that a brand will honor its return policy without any hassle is likelier to speak positively about their experience and recommend the brand within their circles.

Both these principles, social proof and trust, act as psychologically solid levers in transforming customers into brand advocates and understanding them is critical for crafting a successful advocacy strategy.

Adding Colors to the Palette: User-Generated Content and Influencer Marketing

In the digital age, word-of-mouth marketing often takes on new forms like user-generated content and influencer marketing. User-generated content, like reviews, videos, and social media posts, lends authenticity and relatability to your brand's narrative. ASOS's #AsSeenOnMe campaign is a testament to the power of this approach.

Similarly, influencer marketing is a modern take on word-of-mouth. Influencers, due to the trust they have cultivated with their followers, can effectively promote a brand's products or services. The remarkable sales growth Daniel Wellington experienced through its collaboration with Instagram influencers is an inspiring example of this strategy.

Enjoyability and Relatability: The Keys to the Artistic Symphony of Brand Advocacy

Just as a melody can truly resonate when it evokes emotion and reaches deep into one's soul, a parallel can be drawn in the realm of after-sales marketing. In our pursuit of crafting an artistic masterpiece in this space, Nielsen's enlightening report, "Brand building factors for emerging media[3]," provides a harmonious echo. It underlines Enjoyability and Relatability as two of the five essential keys that power recommendation intent, ultimately fostering brand advocacy.

Enjoyability transcends the mere satisfaction derived from a product or service. It is about orchestrating post-purchase experiences that delight, entertain, and bring unexpected joy to customers.

Relatability, in the context of after-sales marketing, calls for tailoring our communication and offers to echo the customers' preferences, needs, and lifestyles. It's about resonating empathy and understanding towards their challenges and desires, thereby forging a deeper bond with the brand that surpasses the functional benefits of our product or service.

Just as a relatable melody can touch one's heart, a brand that echoes understanding and empathy can inspire customers to become vocal advocates. They weave their experiences with the brand into their narratives, effectively recommending us to their circles.

---

3. https://www.nielsen.com/insights/2023/brand-building-factors-for-emerging-media/

These elements form the brushstrokes in the art of after-sales marketing, creating a masterpiece that captivates the audience, inspiring them to become our enthusiastic gallery guides—our cherished brand advocates.

Sketching the Blueprint: Building a Brand Advocacy Program

Creating a brand advocacy program requires careful planning, akin to sketching the blueprint of a painting.

Identifying potential advocates forms the first stroke - these are customers who engage with your brand frequently and show a natural enthusiasm for your offerings. Incentives add color to your sketch, motivating these identified advocates to champion your brand. Equipping them with the right tools, like shareable content or unique referral codes, allows them to spread the word easily.

Public or private appreciation of their efforts acknowledges their contribution, enhancing their connection to the brand.

Regular evaluation and optimization of your program ensure it remains effective and engaging, much like an artist refining their work for maximum impact.

Adding the Finishing Touches: Measuring the Impact

A well-crafted painting deserves critical appraisal, and your word-of-mouth marketing efforts are no different. From using the Net Promoter Score (NPS) to track customer loyalty to monitoring user-generated content, several metrics can help you gauge the effectiveness of your initiatives.

Incorporating Technology: Enhancing the Artform

Technology can amplify your word-of-mouth marketing strategies like an artist leveraging advanced tools to enhance their craft.

CRM systems can help identify potential brand advocates. Email marketing platforms can automate the distribution of referral codes and incentives. Social media platforms enable sharing of user-generated content, and tools like Yotpo can promote positive reviews, leveraging word-of-mouth marketing to reach a larger audience.

Case Studies of Effective Word-of-Mouth Marketing

Examining the work of successful artists can inspire your own creation. Likewise, studying brands that have effectively leveraged word-of-mouth marketing can offer valuable insights. Companies like Tesla, Airbnb, and Dropbox have achieved remarkable success using these strategies.

Case Study 1: Tesla Motors

Tesla Motors provides a brilliant example of effective word-of-mouth marketing. Despite having a virtually non-existent advertising budget, the company's brand advocacy efforts have turned it into a world-renowned brand. Tesla has made a name for itself through innovative products, a charismatic CEO, and, most importantly, delighted customers who advocate for the brand.

The high quality of its electric cars, combined with the unique buying experience and excellent customer service, has led to increased customer satisfaction and advocacy. The Tesla Referral Program, which provides incentives for customers who refer new buyers, has been a successful initiative, transforming their customers into vocal brand advocates and driving new sales.

Case Study 2: Airbnb

Airbnb, the online marketplace for lodging, primarily built its brand through word-of-mouth marketing. They quickly comprehended the power of personal recommendations and developed a referral program.

This program allows current users to invite friends to join Airbnb by offering travel credit to both parties when the referred friend completes their first trip.

The relatability and personal connection associated with staying in someone else's home created stories that customers wanted to share. In this way, Airbnb successfully turned its customers into brand ambassadors.

Case Study 3: Dropbox

Dropbox's exponential growth can be attributed to its successful referral program, a prime example of leveraging word-of-mouth marketing. Dropbox offered free additional storage space as a reward for referring new users. Customers were more motivated to participate because the offer benefited both the referrer and the referee.

As a result, Dropbox saw a dramatic increase in signups, demonstrating the powerful influence of customer advocacy. The company's approach to making referrals easy and beneficial to its customers ultimately made it one of the most well-known file hosting services.

Painting Within the Lines: Ethical Considerations in Word-of-Mouth Marketing

While word-of-mouth marketing can be highly effective, upholding ethical standards is crucial. This includes being transparent about relationships with influencers, not incentivizing or fabricating reviews, and respecting privacy and personal information.

Brands that uphold high ethical standards not only protect their reputation but also build trust and loyalty among their customers, further strengthening their word-of-mouth marketing efforts.

In the chapters ahead, we will explore how we can leverage innovative tools and techniques to enhance our after-sales experiences, creating captivating narratives that inspire our customers to become passionate brand advocates. Through this, we'll amplify our brand's reach and strengthen its credibility and trustworthiness.

Chapter 4: The After-Sales Marketing Symphony: Exploring the Key Tools

IN MUSIC, SEVEN NOTES together create infinite melodies. In painting, we have seven primary colors that, in combination, can create countless shades. In the realm of after-sales marketing, we have seven primary tools that can make a harmonious symphony of customer engagement and satisfaction:

1. Customer Relationship Management (CRM) Systems
2. Email Marketing Platforms
3. Feedback and Survey Tools
4. Social Media Platforms
5. Loyalty Programs
6. Analytics Tools
7. Innovative After-Sales Platforms

Let's examine each of these tools and understand how they can play different yet complementary roles in your after-sales marketing orchestra.

1. Customer Relationship Management (CRM) Systems

CRMS ARE THE BACKBONE of any customer-focused organization. They store valuable customer data, track customer interactions, and help segment customers for personalized marketing. Salesforce, HubSpot, and Zoho are some popular CRMs.

Stages of Customer Journey

Post-Purchase Support:

- Track customer inquiries and complaints, ensuring timely response and resolution.

- Record and analyze product/service issues for improvement.

- Facilitate communication between different departments (sales, customer service, technical support).

Ongoing Engagement:

- Segmentation for targeted marketing and personalized customer experience.

- Management of customer lifecycle stages.

- Track and measure customer engagement metrics.

Advocacy and Referrals:

- Identify potential brand advocates based on customer interaction data.

- Execute referral programs through tracking and rewarding referrals.

- Record customer testimonials for future marketing.

Impact Analysis

Personalization & Customer Perception:

CRM systems collect and analyze customer data to provide personalized experiences, significantly influencing customer perception. A Salesforce study[1] found that 52% of consumers expect offers to be personalized and are likely to switch brands if that need isn't met. CRM systems play a crucial role in delivering this level of personalization.

Improved Retention Rates:

CRM systems dramatically improve retention rates by streamlining communication and ensuring timely and effective service. According to a study by Bain & Company[2], increasing customer retention rates by just 5% can increase profits by up to 95%.

Enhanced Customer Loyalty:

CRM systems can enhance customer loyalty by providing better service and customer experiences. As per Salesforce research[3], 91% of polled customers say they're more likely to make a repeat purchase after a positive experience, and 71% say they've made a purchase decision

---

1. https://www.salesforce.com/news/stories/customer-spending/

2. https://media.bain.com/Images/BB_Prescription_cutting_costs.pdf

3. https://www.salesforce.com/resources/articles/customer-expectations/

based on experience quality, underscoring the significant role that CRM plays in enhancing loyalty.

Predictive Analytics & Customer Lifecycle Management:

CRM systems employ advanced predictive analytics that helps understand customer behavior, preferences, and lifecycle patterns. As demonstrated by a leading airline, as reported by McKinsey[4], using these systems led to an 800% uplift in satisfaction and a 60% reduction in churn for priority customers.

Increasing Revenue:

CRM systems directly impact a company's bottom line. A report by Nucleus Research[5] suggests that the average return on investment (ROI) for CRM is $8.71 for every dollar spent.

Boosting Customer Satisfaction:

CRM systems can significantly boost customer satisfaction by providing timely service, personalized interactions, and a seamless customer experience. An illustration of this is found in consumer behavior trends: 78% of customers are willing to go out of their way for a company that provides better customer service, and 74% would switch to a competing brand if they found out that they provide superior customer service, as noted in a report by SuperOffice[6].

Pitfalls to Avoid and Corresponding Best Practices

Pitfall: Incomplete or Inconsistent Data Entry

---

4. https://www.mckinsey.com/capabilities/growth-marketing-and-sales/our-insights/prediction-the-future-of-cx

5. https://nucleusresearch.com/wp-content/uploads/2018/05/o128-CRM-pays-back-8.71-for-every-dollar-spent.pdf

6. https://www.superoffice.com/blog/measure-customer-satisfaction/

Best Practice: Maintaining a complete and uniform database is crucial for understanding customer interactions and behavior. Implementing mandatory fields and consistent data entry guidelines can help ensure data completeness and consistency.

Pitfall: Neglecting Staff Training

Best Practice: Training your team to use the CRM effectively is critical to maximizing its benefits. This includes not just technical training but also helping them understand the value of CRM in improving customer relationships and sales efficiency.

Pitfall: Lack of Integration with Other Systems

Best Practice: Your CRM should be integrated with other vital systems in your organization, like your marketing automation platform and service software. This provides a holistic view of the customer across all touchpoints.

Pitfall: Ignoring CRM Analytics

Best Practice: CRMs often come equipped with analytical tools that can provide insightful data on customer behavior and sales trends. Regularly reviewing and acting on this data can improve your customer strategy and boost sales.

Pitfall: Viewing CRM as a Purely Sales Tool

Best Practice: CRM isn't just about sales – it's about building and managing customer relationships at every stage. This includes marketing, service, feedback, and more. Adopt a holistic approach to using your CRM.

Pitfall: Not Updating the CRM Regularly

Best Practice: Keeping your CRM updated with the latest customer data, interactions, and notes is essential. This ensures that all team members can access the most recent information, which can guide their interactions and strategies.

Pitfall: Not Using the CRM to Improve the Customer Experience

Best Practice: Use the CRM to anticipate customer needs and personalize their experience. With a wealth of customer data at your fingertips, you can personalize your communications and offers, ultimately enhancing customer satisfaction and loyalty.

2. Email Marketing Platforms

THESE TOOLS ENABLE you to send personalized emails to your customers. They allow you to segment your customer base and send targeted messages, increasing engagement and sales. Examples include MailChimp, Constant Contact, and GetResponse.

Stages of Customer Journey

Post-Purchase Support:

- Send automated confirmation and thank-you emails.

- Deliver instruction guides or product usage tips.

- Notify customers about warranty and service schedules.

Ongoing Engagement:

- Share regular newsletters with valuable content.

- Promote new products, updates, and offers.

- Personalized emails based on customer interests and behavior.

Advocacy and Referrals:

- Request feedback and reviews via email.

- Run referral programs by encouraging sharing via email.

- Acknowledge and reward customer loyalty through emails.

Impact Analysis

Enhanced Customer Relationships:

Email marketing platforms allow businesses to maintain regular contact with customers, providing them with valuable information tailored to their interests. According to the Adobe study[1], a significant portion of respondents (56% for work, 60% for personal) expressed a preference for receiving offers via email over other marketing channels, indicating the vital role email marketing plays in fostering brand loyalty.

Customer Re-engagement:

Email marketing platforms remain an effective tool for re-engaging lapsed customers. According to the report by Omnisend[2], lapsed-purchaser messages held a robust conversion rate of 21.3%. This statistic emphasizes the power of tailored email campaigns in reigniting customer interest and fostering re-engagement.

Customer Loyalty:

Email marketing can play a pivotal role in cultivating customer loyalty. Businesses can foster a strong bond with their customers by delivering personalized content that adds value and acknowledging milestones with special offers or gifts. According to Campaign Monitor[3], personalized email campaigns can drive a 760% increase in email revenue.

Feedback and Insights:

---

1. https://business.adobe.com/blog/perspectives/if-you-think-email-is-dead-think-again

2. https://www.omnisend.com/resources/reports/ecommerce-statistics-report-2021/

3. https://www.campaignmonitor.com/resources/guides/email-marketing-new-rules/

Email marketing platforms can also provide businesses with valuable feedback and insights. By tracking metrics like open rates, click-through rates, and conversion rates, companies can gain a deeper understanding of their customers' behaviors and preferences, enabling them to refine their marketing strategies effectively.

Pitfalls to Avoid and Corresponding Best Practices

Pitfall: Ignoring Personalization

Best Practice: Emails should be tailored to the preferences and behaviors of individual customers. Personalization makes marketing messages more relevant and interesting to recipients, increasing the likelihood of engagement.

Pitfall: Failing to Segment Your Audience

Best Practice: Email lists should be segmented based on the different stages of the customer journey, demographics, and customer behavior. Segmented email campaigns are typically more successful because they deliver more relevant content to different groups of subscribers.

Pitfall: Neglecting Mobile Optimization

Best Practice: It's crucial to ensure that emails are optimized for mobile devices. Many consumers now check their emails on their phones, so if an email isn't mobile-optimized, it may not display properly or be easy to read, decreasing engagement.

Pitfall: Not Analyzing Campaign Performance

Best Practice: The analytic tools provided by the email marketing platform should be used to assess the performance of campaigns. By measuring key metrics like open rate, click-through rate, and conversion rate, strategies can be adjusted based on these insights for better performance in future campaigns.

Pitfall: Overlooking GDPR Compliance

Best Practice: It's vital to ensure email marketing practices are GDPR compliant. This includes getting explicit consent from subscribers before sending marketing emails, giving them the option to unsubscribe at any point, and protecting their data privacy. Non-compliance can lead to severe penalties.

3. Feedback and Survey Tools

TOOLS LIKE SURVEYMONKEY, Typeform, and Google Forms help you gather customer feedback and gauge satisfaction levels. They can also aid in improving your product/service based on customer insights.

Stages of Customer Journey

Post-Purchase Support:

- Collect feedback on customer support experiences.

- Understand product/service issues or customer pain points.

- Conduct post-purchase satisfaction surveys.

Ongoing Engagement:

- Conduct regular customer surveys to gather insights and show customers that their opinion matters.

- Use survey data for continuous improvement and personalization.

Advocacy and Referrals:

- Ask for reviews and ratings through surveys.

- Leverage positive survey results in marketing and social proof.

Impact Analysis

Enhanced Understanding of Customer Needs:

Survey tools give businesses a structured mechanism to capture the voice of the customer. They help companies to gain insights into what customers truly want, their unmet needs, and areas where the product or service can be improved. According to a Microsoft report[1], 89% of consumers want to be heard and are eager to share their experience with the brand.

Improved Product Development:

Feedback tools can provide real-time information about what's working and what's not about a particular product or service. This feedback can be instrumental in driving product development and improvements. For instance, when DHL integrated customer feedback into their supply chain improvement strategy, they developed a drone delivery service, the Parcelcopter. As reported by Wonderflow[2], this integration led to customer satisfaction exceeding 80%, and on-time delivery performance reaching 97% globally.

Brand Reputation Management:

Companies can use feedback and survey tools to monitor and manage their brand's reputation. Timely identification and resolution of negative feedback can prevent potentially damaging situations. A survey by BrightLocal[3] found that 76% of consumers trust online reviews as much as personal recommendations, highlighting the importance of managing online feedback.

Increased Customer Engagement:

---

1. https://info.microsoft.com/ww-landing-global-state-of-customer-service.html

2. https://www.wonderflow.ai/blog/customer-feedback-with-product-development/

3. https://www.brightlocal.com/research/local-consumer-review-survey/

Asking customers for feedback shows them their opinion is valued and can increase customer engagement. According to Apptentive[4], by creating customer feedback loops and proactively engaging, they have helped their customers boost engagement rates to 23%, reaching over 20 times more consumers than the conventional rate.

Pitfalls to Avoid and Corresponding Best Practices

Pitfall: Overcomplicated Surveys

Best Practice: Keep your surveys concise, clear, and focused. The longer and more complex your survey is, the less likely customers will complete it.

Pitfall: Ignoring Open-Ended Questions

Best Practice: Include a mix of close-ended and open-ended questions. The latter allows customers to express their opinions in their own words, revealing insights that might be missed in a close-ended question.

Pitfall: Overlooking Negative Feedback

Best Practice: Consider all feedback, especially negative ones. This provides an opportunity to address issues and make necessary improvements. Remember, customers who take time to give negative feedback are often the ones who care about your business the most.

Pitfall: Lack of Follow-Up

Best Practice: Show your customers that their feedback matters. Follow up with them, communicate what actions have been taken based on their feedback, and thank them for helping improve your business.

Pitfall: Not Analyzing and Acting on Feedback

4. https://mobile.alchemer.com/2020-mobile-customer-engagement-benchmark-report

Best Practice: Feedback is only valuable if you analyze it and use it to make informed business decisions. Use feedback to identify patterns, trends, and areas for improvement.

Pitfall: Not Testing the Survey Before Sending

Best Practice: Always test your surveys before sending them out. This helps you identify any errors or issues that may affect the survey's usability or the accuracy of the data collected.

Pitfall: Asking Leading or Biased Questions

Best Practice: Ensure your questions are unbiased and open-ended to get the most accurate and genuine responses.

4. Social Media Platforms

FACEBOOK, INSTAGRAM, Twitter, LinkedIn, and other social media platforms are crucial for maintaining a relationship with your customers post-purchase. They allow for immediate interaction and sharing of valuable content.

Stages of Customer Journey

Post-Purchase Support:

- Respond to customer inquiries and complaints on social media.

- Share product usage tips and hacks.

- Provide real-time updates on customer support issues.

Ongoing Engagement:

- Share engaging content and updates regularly.

- Organize social media contests, quizzes, and live events.

- Personalize customer experiences through direct messaging.

Advocacy and Referrals:

- Encourage customers to share their positive experiences and reviews on social media.

- Run referral programs and encourage sharing on social media.

- Recognize and reward customer loyalty on public platforms.

Impact Analysis

Brand Awareness and Visibility:

Social media platforms offer businesses the chance to increase their brand visibility significantly. According to GlobalWebIndex[1], 54% of social browsers use social media to research products, showing the potential for sales through social media platforms.

Improved Customer Service:

Social media enables companies to interact with customers in real time, allowing for prompt resolution of queries and complaints. A survey by Sprout Social[2] indicates that 74% of consumers have used social media in some way to communicate directly with a brand.

Customer Insight and Targeting:

Through social media analytics, businesses can gain valuable insights into their customers' interests, behaviors, and preferences, enabling them to target their marketing efforts effectively.

Increased Traffic and Sales:

By sharing content and engaging with followers on social media, companies can drive traffic to their websites and increase sales. When consumers follow a brand on social, Sprout's research[3] shows that 89% will buy from that brand and 75% of consumers will increase their spending with that brand.

---

1. https://www.gwi.com/reports/social-2020

2. https://media.sproutsocial.com/uploads/2020-Sprout-Social-Index-Above-and-Beyond.pdf

3. https://media.sproutsocial.com/uploads/2020-Sprout-Social-Index-Above-and-Beyond.pdf

Pitfalls to Avoid and Corresponding Best Practices

Pitfall: Not Having a Defined Social Media Strategy

Best Practice: Define your social media strategy before you start posting. This includes your goals, target audience, key performance indicators, and content calendar.

Pitfall: Ignoring or Deleting Negative Comments

Best Practice: Address negative comments in a professional and timely manner. Apologize if necessary and take the conversation offline if it becomes too complicated.

Pitfall: Infrequent or Inconsistent Posting

Best Practice: Maintain a regular posting schedule. Consistency is critical to maintaining your audience's interest and engagement.

Pitfall: Over-Promotion

Best Practice: Follow the 80/20 rule – 80% of your content should be informative, entertaining, or inspiring, and only 20% should be promotional.

Pitfall: Not Engaging with Your Audience

Best Practice: Social media is a two-way communication platform. Make sure to engage with your audience by responding to comments, liking their posts, and asking for their opinions.

Pitfall: Not Utilizing All Platform Features

Best Practice: Most social media platforms offer a range of features for businesses, such as analytics, targeted advertising, and story features. Utilize these features to reach a larger audience and gain more insights about your customers.

Pitfall: Posting the Same Content on All Platforms

Best Practice: Tailor your content for each platform. What works on Facebook may only work on something other than Instagram or LinkedIn. Understand the nuances of each platform and create content accordingly.

5. Loyalty Programs

LOYALTY PROGRAMS LIKE points systems, tier programs, and referral programs incentivize customers to repeat purchases and recommend your brand to others. Tools for managing these programs include Yotpo, Smile.io, and LoyaltyLion.

Stages of Customer Journey

Post-Purchase Support:

- Use the loyalty program to offer exclusive support benefits like priority service.

- Reward customers with loyalty points for providing valuable feedback.

Ongoing Engagement:

- Use the loyalty program to incentivize repeat purchases.

- Offer personalized rewards based on customer preferences.

Advocacy and Referrals:

- Reward customers for referrals through the loyalty program.

- Leverage loyalty program data to identify and nurture brand advocates.

Impact Analysis

Boosts Customer Engagement:

Loyalty programs reward customers for their purchases and engage them in a way that cultivates a deeper relationship with the brand. By offering customers exclusive content, experiences, or the opportunity to be part of a community, brands can significantly increase engagement rates. According to Yotpo's report[1], loyalty programs make 60% of global shoppers more loyal to a brand, underscoring the effectiveness of these programs in boosting engagement.

Higher Customer Lifetime Value:

Loyalty programs can significantly increase customer lifetime value (CLV) by encouraging repeat purchases and increasing the average order value. A report by Bond Brand Loyalty[2] indicates that 66% of consumers modify the amount they spend to maximize points, signifying the potential for increased revenue per customer.

Competitive Advantage:

In a market crowded with similar products or services, loyalty programs can serve as a differentiating factor that can sway customers to choose your brand over others.

Customer Data and Personalization:

Loyalty programs often require customers to share personal information, providing valuable data for personalization and targeted marketing efforts. Bond Brand Loyalty's report[3] reveals that credit card programs that achieve high levels of personalization along the member lifecycle experience a $196 lift in spend on card, per member, per month.

---

1. https://www.yotpo.com/the-state-of-brand-loyalty-2022/emotional-loyalty-is-in-and-has-to-be-earned/

2. https://info.bondbrandloyalty.com/the-2016-bond-loyalty-report-press-release-us

3. https://info.bondbrandloyalty.com/tlr-2020

Pitfalls to Avoid and Corresponding Best Practices

Pitfall: Making the Loyalty Program Too Complex

Best Practice: Keep your loyalty program simple and easy to understand. The easier it is for customers to understand, the more likely they are to participate.

Pitfall: Offering Irrelevant Rewards

Best Practice: Offer rewards that your customers value. This could be discounts, exclusive products, or unique experiences. Use customer data and feedback to determine what rewards would be most enticing.

Pitfall: Not Communicating the Benefits Clearly

Best Practice: Clearly communicate the benefits of the loyalty program to your customers. Highlight how they can earn and redeem points, what the rewards are, and any additional perks or benefits.

Pitfall: Not Analyzing and Adapting the Program

Best Practice: Regularly analyze the performance of your loyalty program. Look at metrics like participation rate, the average spend of loyalty program members vs non-members, and redemption rate. Use this data to make improvements to your program.

Pitfall: Not Recognizing and Rewarding Your Most Loyal Customers

Best Practice: Create tiers in your loyalty program to recognize and reward your most loyal customers. This not only encourages them to spend more but also makes them feel valued.

Pitfall: Failing to Personalize the Program

Best Practice: Personalize your loyalty program as much as possible. This could be as simple as addressing customers by their name in communications or as complex as offering personalized rewards based on purchasing behavior.

Pitfall: Not Promoting Your Loyalty Program

Best Practice: Promote your loyalty program through all your marketing channels. Make sure your customers know about it and understand the benefits of joining.

Pitfall: Neglecting the Customer Experience

Best Practice: Ensure the loyalty program adds to the customer experience rather than detracting from it. It should be easy to join, participate in, and redeem rewards. If the process is simple and smooth, customers may continue the program.

6. Analytics Tools

TOOLS LIKE GOOGLE ANALYTICS, Mixpanel, and Tableau help you track and analyze customer behavior on your website or app, giving you insights to refine your after-sales strategy.

Stages of Customer Journey

Post-Purchase Support:

- Analyze customer behavior data to identify and address support issues.

- Measure customer satisfaction and support effectiveness.

Ongoing Engagement:

- Use data insights to refine and personalize engagement strategies.

- Measure and track engagement metrics over time.

Advocacy and Referrals:

- Identify potential advocates based on engagement data.

- Measure the success of referral programs and refine strategies.

Impact Analysis

Enhanced Decision Making:

Analytics tools enable businesses to make data-driven decisions by providing insights into customer behavior, product performance, and market trends. In fact, according to the report by MicroStrategy[1], a striking 94% of organizations believe data and analytics are crucial to their business growth and digital transformation.

Improved Marketing ROI:

Analytics tools allow businesses to measure the effectiveness of their marketing campaigns, identify high-performing channels, and optimize marketing spend. According to a study by Nucleus Research[2], businesses that invest in analytics tools see, on average, a return of $13.01 for every dollar they spend.

Predictive Analysis for Customer Trends:

With the help of advanced machine learning algorithms, analytics tools can predict future customer behavior, enabling businesses to anticipate customer needs and adjust their strategies accordingly.

Identifying Bottlenecks in the Customer Journey:

Analytics tools can help businesses identify stages in the customer journey where customers drop off, allowing them to improve these areas and enhance the overall customer experience.

Pitfalls to Avoid and Corresponding Best Practices

Pitfall: Focusing Only on Vanity Metrics

Best Practice: Instead of concentrating solely on vanity metrics (like page views or followers), focus on actionable metrics (like engagement

---

1. https://www3.microstrategy.com/getmedia/db67a6c7-0bc5-41fa-82a9-bb14ec6868d6/2020-Global-State-of-Enterprise-Analytics.pdf

2. https://nucleusresearch.com/research/single/analytics-pays-back-13-01-for-every-dollar-spent/

rate or customer churn rate) that provide insights about customer behavior and can guide your marketing strategies.

Pitfall: Ignoring the Customer Journey

Best Practice: Use analytics tools to understand and visualize the entire customer journey. This can help identify friction points, engagement opportunities, and strategies for improving customer retention and advocacy.

Pitfall: Not Segmenting Your Data

Best Practice: Segment your data to gain deeper insights. This could be based on demographics, customer behavior, or other relevant factors. Segmentation can reveal trends and patterns not visible in the aggregated data.

Pitfall: Misinterpreting the Data

Best Practice: Ensure that your team has the necessary skills to interpret the data accurately. Misinterpretations can lead to misguided decisions and strategies.

Pitfall: Not Leveraging Real-time Data

Best Practice: Use real-time data to make immediate decisions. This could be particularly useful in managing customer relationships and personalizing your marketing efforts.

Pitfall: Not Aligning Your Analytics with Business Goals

Best Practice: Align your analytics strategy with your business goals. Your key performance indicators (KPIs) should directly reflect your business objectives.

Pitfall: Not Integrating Data from All Channels

Best Practice: Integrate data from all customer touchpoints to view the customer journey comprehensively. This can help you understand how different channels contribute to your goals and how they interact with each other.

Pitfall: Not Ensuring Data Accuracy

Best Practice: Regularly check and clean your data to ensure its accuracy. Only accurate data can lead to correct insights and decisions.

7. Innovative After-Sales Platforms

AS WE JOURNEY FURTHER into the digital age, we continually witness the birth of innovative platforms revolutionizing the way we approach after-sales marketing. These cutting-edge tools harness the power of technology to create an elevated customer experience, enabling businesses to keep their clientele engaged, loyal, and invested in the brand even after the transaction is complete.

From AI-driven customer interaction platforms to interactive content generators, from social media listening tools to predictive analytics solutions, we will see how the landscape of after-sales marketing is rapidly evolving.

AI-Driven Customer Interaction Tools:

Platforms like Ada or Intercom use artificial intelligence to automate and personalize customer interactions across different channels. These tools are becoming pivotal in after-sales marketing to ensure a seamless customer experience and round-the-clock customer service.

Augmented Reality (AR) Experiences:

Augmented reality is enhancing the way customers interact with products and services post-purchase. For instance, IKEA's AR app allows customers to virtually place furniture in their homes to see how it fits and looks, providing a unique after-sales service that enhances product satisfaction and reduces returns.

Interactive Content Platforms:

Tools such as Apester or Outgrow enable businesses to create interactive content such as quizzes, polls, and videos. These engaging content forms are used in after-sales marketing to keep the customer engaged, gather feedback, and offer personalized recommendations.

Social Media Listening Tools:

Platforms like Hootsuite or Mention provide real-time insights into customer sentiment and brand mentions across social media platforms. These tools are invaluable in after-sales marketing, allowing businesses to respond to customer inquiries or complaints promptly, capitalize on positive reviews, and manage brand reputation.

eCards:

Companies like igreetu Bespoke offer a unique way of keeping customers engaged post-purchase. Customers can send free eCards featuring elements of your corporate identity, creating a personalized experience and encouraging word-of-mouth marketing.

Predictive Analytics Tools:

Solutions such as Evergage or Adobe Analytics harness machine learning and data analysis to anticipate customer behavior and needs based on past interactions. In after-sales marketing, this can facilitate personalized interactions and proactive customer service, thus enhancing customer satisfaction and loyalty.

Bonus: A Toolkit for Your After-Sales Journey

AS YOU TURN THE PAGES of this book, we hope you have been able to grasp the fascinating world of after-sales marketing. To enrich your journey and help you apply these concepts to your business, we have a pleasant surprise for you!

We have crafted an exclusive After-Sales Marketing Notion Template designed to guide you as you navigate through the strategies and tactics outlined in this book. This powerful tool is your digital companion, giving you a hands-on, practical approach to implementing the ideas and principles shared on these pages.

The template provides a structured workspace to plan, organize, and track your after-sales initiatives. From customer segmentation to retention strategies and crafting personalized customer experiences to measuring the impact of your efforts - this Notion Template has you covered.

Access to this template is complimentary to purchasing this book, adding value to your reading experience. It's our way of saying thank you for embarking on this journey with us, and we trust it will be a valuable resource as you transform your after-sales marketing approach.

To access your FREE After-Sales Marketing Notion Template, visit this link: https://affiliate.notion.so/after-sales-marketing.

Once inside, you'll find step-by-step instructions to guide you in making the most of this tool.

We designed this surprise with you, the reader, in mind, ensuring you have an actionable way to implement the insights from this book. This extra touch will help further your understanding and application of after-sales marketing, propelling your business to new heights of customer satisfaction and loyalty.

Remember, after-sales marketing is not a one-time event but a continuous learning, implementing, testing, and refining process. With this Notion Template, we're honored to be a part of your journey.

In the upcoming chapter, we'll delve deeper into how we can leverage these tools and techniques to craft compelling after-sales experiences that resonate deeply with customers, turning each interaction into a vibrant brushstroke in our masterpiece of marketing.

Chapter 5: The Masterpiece Unveiled: Creating Lasting Impressions

EVERY INTERACTION WITH a customer post-sale is an opportunity to create a lasting impression, to add another layer of color to our masterpiece. The key to making such impressions is designing compelling after-sales narratives and experiences that resonate deeply with customers.

Designing Compelling After-Sales Narratives

A well-crafted narrative, in its essence, is a strategically designed tale that unfolds over time. Its goal is to weave a story connecting your customers to your brand, products, and values. It paints a picture that goes beyond a mere transaction and immerses your customers in an experience that is uniquely yours.

As an after-sales strategy, narratives are incredibly compelling. They offer an opportunity to tell the customer they've joined a story that will continue to evolve. It's not just about the product they purchased but the community they've become a part of, the mission they are now supporting, and the journey they've embarked upon.

The key to successful after-sales narratives lies in consistency and personal relevance. A story must be consistently relayed across all your after-sales interactions, from email follow-ups to customer service.

On the other hand, personal relevance means the story must resonate personally with your customers. It should echo their values, aspirations, and experiences. This makes the narrative immersive, relatable, and engaging.

Crafting Personalized Experiences that Deepen the Emotional Connection

Crafting personalized experiences means going beyond the one-size-fits-all approach. It involves understanding your customer's needs, preferences, and experiences, then tailoring your after-sales interactions to meet these individual needs.

From personalized emails that address the customer by name and reference their specific purchases to product recommendations that consider their buying history and preferences - each interaction should make the customer feel recognized and unique.

These personalized experiences also extend to how you solve problems and handle complaints. Tailoring your problem-solving approaches to the customer shows you see and respect their unique situation. This helps transform potentially negative experiences into opportunities to demonstrate your commitment to your customers, deepening the emotional bond between the customer and your brand.

Remember, in the end, people crave connections. By crafting compelling narratives and personalized experiences in your after-sales interactions, you can foster a meaningful and emotional connection with your customers that fuels loyalty and advocacy.

As we dive into the intricate world of after-sales marketing, we discover various strategies that blend the art of storytelling, the power of technology, and the depth of human emotions.

These are not standalone techniques but a symphony of interlaced approaches, each playing its part in a harmonious rendition to retain customers, enhance brand loyalty, and inspire advocacy.

Strategy 1: The Journey Continues

REMIND CUSTOMERS THAT their purchase is not the end of their journey with your brand but the beginning of a new chapter.

Strategic Overview

The primary goal of this strategy is to foster a long-term relationship with the customer by continually engaging them beyond the point of purchase. This strategy will transform the purchasing process from a transactional encounter into an ongoing journey with your brand.

Key Tasks

Follow-Up Communication:

Implement a follow-up communication system that involves timely check-ins with the customer post-purchase.

Value-Adding Content:

Curate content that will add value to the customer's experience with the product or service. This could be in the form of tips, how-tos, advice, stories, and any other content that enhances the use of your product.

Progress Tracking Tools:

Provide tools to customers that allow them to track their progress or achievements with your product or service.

Recommended Tools

- This strategy would best utilize Email Marketing Platforms for regular, automated follow-up communication.

- CRM Systems would be essential for managing individual customer information, their journey, and the communications sent.

- Analytics Tools would help track the effectiveness of the communications and improve based on customer responses.

Customer Psychology After-Purchase

Post-purchase, customers often experience an emotional high from acquiring a new product or service. However, this feeling can quickly deflate once the novelty wears off.

You can prolong and capitalize on this post-purchase positivity by reminding customers that their purchase is just the beginning of an exciting journey.

Furthermore, by continuing to engage customers and add value to their experience, you can stave off buyer's remorse and promote a feeling of satisfaction and loyalty.

Improving Retention, Loyalty, and Brand Advocacy

Regular follow-up communication keeps your brand fresh in the minds of customers. When you consistently provide valuable content and support, customers feel acknowledged and appreciated, improving retention and loyalty.

Additionally, by personalizing the experience and championing the customer's progress, you're creating an emotional connection that builds loyalty and turns customers into brand ambassadors.

Examples of Application

THE ART OF AFTER-SALES MARKETING

A Fitness Equipment Company:

After a customer purchases a treadmill, the company could send regular follow-up emails with workout plans, fitness tips, and motivational stories. They could provide a tool to track the customer's fitness progress and celebrate milestones, thus intertwining the customer's fitness journey with their brand.

A Software Company:

After selling a project management tool to a company, the software company could send regular tips and tricks on maximizing the use of their software. They could provide a personalized dashboard to track the company's progress and productivity improvements.

A Cooking Utensil Brand:

After a customer purchases a premium set of cooking pans, the brand could send regular follow-up communications with new recipes to try, maintenance tips for the pans, and exclusive content from renowned chefs. They could provide a platform for customers to share their culinary creations, fostering a community around their brand.

Strategy 2: Behind the Scenes

GIVE CUSTOMERS AN EXCLUSIVE peek behind the scenes. This could involve sharing stories about how their product was made, introducing them to the people behind the innovation, or sharing insights about your company's mission and values.

Strategic Overview

The "Behind the Scenes" strategy aims to establish transparency and authenticity, fostering a sense of trust and connection between the brand and its customers.

By granting customers a glimpse into the inner workings of your company or the journey of their purchased product, you humanize your brand, demystify your process, and deepen customer engagement.

Key Tasks

Content Creation:

Develop content that showcases the behind-the-scenes processes of your company, the making of your products, the people behind your brand, or the values that drive your operations.

Storytelling:

Use storytelling to make your behind-the-scenes content engaging and relatable. Remember, the goal is to connect with your customers emotionally, not just to provide information.

Distribution:

Share this content through appropriate channels – this could be email, social media, your company blog, or even a dedicated section on your website.

Recommended Tools

- Social Media Platforms are perfect for showcasing behind-the-scenes content in an engaging and easily sharable format.

- Email Marketing Platforms can be used for sending this exclusive content to your customers.

- CRM Systems can help track customer engagement with this content, and

- Analytics Tools can provide insights into the effectiveness of your communication.

Customer Psychology After-Purchase

Consumers increasingly value transparency and authenticity from the brands they choose. Offering a peek behind the scenes caters to this desire, deepening their trust in your brand. It reassures them about the quality of your products and gives them a sense of participating in your company's story.

Improving Retention, Loyalty, and Brand Advocacy

Transparency builds trust, and trust is vital to retaining customers. Letting customers in on your company's processes, values, and people creates a stronger bond with them, improving their loyalty to your brand.

Plus, consumers love to share fascinating insights or feel-good stories about the brands they like, so this strategy can naturally turn your customers into brand advocates.

Examples of Application

A Handmade Jewelry Brand:

This brand could share stories about how their jewelry is made, including the sourcing of the materials, the inspiration behind each piece, and the artisans who create them. They could even share video clips of the jewelry-making process on their social media platforms.

A Coffee Roastery:

The roastery could give customers insights into their coffee sourcing process, introducing them to the farmers they partner with and explaining their fair-trade practices. They could share a blog series detailing their journey from bean to cup, giving customers an appreciation for the work that goes into their daily cup of coffee.

A Tech Company:

After a customer purchases a software product, the company could send them a series of emails introducing them to the team behind the product, explaining their design and development process, and sharing the company's mission and values. This gives a face to the brand and helps the customer feel connected to the product and company.

Strategy 3: Celebrating Success

CELEBRATE YOUR CUSTOMERS' success with your product. For example, a software company could showcase case studies of how different customers have used their software to achieve their goals. Not only does this provide social proof, but it also makes customers feel valued and appreciated.

Strategic Overview

The "Celebrating Success" strategy centers around acknowledging and applauding how customers use your product or service to achieve their goals. This strategy establishes a deep sense of shared success and appreciation, empowering your customers and driving their loyalty toward your brand.

Key Tasks

Identify Success Stories:

Keep track of the wins and accomplishments of your customers as they use your products or services. These could be professional milestones, personal achievements, or even more minor victories that they attribute to your brand.

Create Case Studies:

Document these success stories as case studies. Make sure to capture the problem, solution, and outcome in detail, highlighting how your product played a role in the customer's success.

Share and Celebrate:

Share these case studies on appropriate platforms, and celebrate these achievements. This could be as part of your marketing content, within your community, or even at dedicated events.

Recommended Tools

- CRM Systems will play a vital role in identifying customers who have achieved significant milestones using your product.

- Social Media and Email Marketing Platforms will be instrumental in sharing and celebrating these success stories.

- Analytics Tools can help gauge the impact of these stories on your audience and adjust your strategy accordingly.

Customer Psychology After-Purchase

After making a purchase, customers look for validation that they made the right decision. Celebrating their success provides this validation and enhances their perception of the product's value. It makes them feel noticed, appreciated, and connected to your brand, deepening their post-purchase satisfaction.

Improving Retention, Loyalty, and Brand Advocacy

Celebrating customer success stories demonstrates that you care about your customers' outcomes, which fosters customer loyalty and improves retention. Furthermore, these stories provide social proof, which can attract potential customers and reinforce the value of your product. This strategy also encourages brand advocacy as satisfied customers often share their success stories within their networks.

Examples of Application

A Language Learning App:

The company could regularly feature users who've reached language proficiency using their app. They could share these stories in their newsletter and social media, celebrating these achievements and inspiring others to pursue their language learning goals.

A Project Management Software Company:

The company could publish case studies showcasing how different teams have used their software to streamline workflows and achieve project goals. This could be shared on their blog and social media, reinforcing the software's value proposition.

A Fitness Brand:

The brand could feature these stories on its platform after customers achieve significant milestones, such as completing a marathon or reaching a personal fitness goal. This could be supplemented with a personalized congratulatory email or a special offer to celebrate their achievement, further enhancing the brand-customer relationship.

Strategy 4: Surprise and Delight

CONSIDER SENDING SURPRISE gifts or perks to your loyal customers. These unexpected gestures can create a strong emotional connection. For instance, an online retailer could send a personalized discount coupon to a customer on their birthday and a branded eCards.

Strategic Overview

The "Surprise and Delight" strategy is about exceeding customer expectations by providing unexpected value, rewards, or experiences. The surprise element evokes strong positive emotions, leading to an enhanced perception of your brand and an emotional connection.

Key Tasks

Identify Opportunities:

Look for occasions or milestones where you can pleasantly surprise your customers. This could be a customer's birthday, the anniversary of their first purchase, or even random acts of kindness.

Plan Surprises:

Prepare thoughtful gifts or perks that resonate with your customers. This could include personalized coupons or discounts, exclusive content, or physical presents.

Execute Delightfully:

Engagingly deliver these surprises. The presentation is as essential as the surprise itself. Ensure your wonder feels personal and exclusive to each customer.

Recommended Tools

- CRM Systems will be crucial in tracking customer data and identifying opportunities to surprise your customers.

- Email Marketing and Innovative After-Sales Platforms like eCards are great for delivering these surprises in a personalized and engaging manner.

Customer Psychology After-Purchase

After a purchase, customers generally expect a smooth and efficient after-sales service. However, unexpected positive gestures like surprises and gifts can induce pleasure and appreciation, leading to a deeper emotional connection with your brand.

Improving Retention, Loyalty, and Brand Advocacy

Surprise gifts or perks can lead to increased customer satisfaction and loyalty. They can transform regular customer interaction into a memorable experience, encouraging repeat purchases and long-term commitment. Moreover, delighted customers will likely share their positive experiences within their networks, acting as brand ambassadors.

Examples of Application

A Subscription Box Service:

To celebrate a customer's one-year subscription anniversary, the company could include an extra surprise gift and a personalized thank you note in their next box.

An Online Bookstore:

On a customer's birthday, the bookstore could send a personalized email with a special birthday discount and a recommendation for a book based on their past purchases.

A Software Company:

The company could offer free premium features to loyal customers for a limited time as a surprise, appreciating their continuous support. They could send this surprise through an exclusive email or in-app notification.

Strategy 5: Tailored Support

OFFER SUPPORT THAT is tailored to each customer's needs or preferences. For instance, a company selling gardening equipment could provide personalized gardening tips based on the customer's purchase history and geographical location.

Strategic Overview

The "Tailored Support" strategy is about providing after-sales support specifically tailored to each customer's unique needs or preferences. This strategy fosters a deep understanding of customers, demonstrating that the brand values and prioritizes their individual requirements.

Key Tasks

Understand Customers:

Collect and analyze customer data to understand their needs, preferences, and behaviors. This includes their purchase history, interactions with your brand, and feedback.

Personalize Support:

Use these insights to offer support that is unique to each customer. This could involve customized tips, advice, or solutions based on their specific context.

Maintain Consistency:

Ensure consistent and continuous personalization. This isn't a one-time effort but rather a long-term commitment to understanding and addressing each customer's evolving needs.

Recommended Tools

- CRM Systems are critical for collecting and analyzing customer data.

- Email Marketing and Social Media Platforms can deliver personalized support.

- Feedback and Survey Tools help understand whether the personalized support is effective or needs modifications.

Customer Psychology After-Purchase

Post-purchase, customers are often in need of guidance to extract maximum value from their purchase. Personalized support that addresses their specific needs can significantly enhance their experience, reducing anxiety and boosting confidence in your brand.

Improving Retention, Loyalty, and Brand Advocacy

Tailored support reinforces customers' perception that they are valued, increasing customer satisfaction, loyalty, and brand advocacy. By showing that you understand and care about their needs, you encourage them to continue doing business with you and recommend your brand to others.

Examples of Application

A Fitness Equipment Company:

The company could provide customers with personalized training plans and tips based on their fitness goals, the equipment they've purchased, and their previous training experience.

An E-commerce Platform:

It could offer personalized product care tips and troubleshooting guides based on a customer's purchase history.

A Gardening Equipment Company:

The company could provide customers with gardening advice tailored to their specific location, soil type, and the plants they've purchased. This can be delivered via personalized emails or through a customized section on their website or app.

Strategy 6: Co-creation

INVOLVE CUSTOMERS IN the creation process. This could involve asking customers for input on new product designs or inviting them to share their ideas and experiences in a community forum. This makes customers feel valued and deepens their emotional investment in your brand.

Strategic Overview

The "Co-creation" strategy involves incorporating customers into your brand's creative and developmental process. It underscores the importance of a brand's commitment to fostering a symbiotic relationship with its customers rather than treating them as mere consumers.

Key Tasks

Create Open Channels of Communication:

Build platforms where customers can express their ideas and insights about your products or services.

Involve Customers in Design and Development:

Encourage customers to contribute ideas for new products or improvements to existing ones.

Implement Feedback:

Show customers their input is valued by implementing viable suggestions and acknowledging their contribution.

Recommended Tools

• Social Media Platforms, Feedback, and Survey Tools are vital in gathering customer insights.

• CRM Systems can help manage customer data and feedback effectively.

• Innovative After-Sales Platforms like community forums can be used for customer interaction and co-creation processes.

Customer Psychology After-Purchase

Once customers purchase a product, they invest not only money but also emotions into it. By involving them in the creation process, they feel more attached to the brand, fostering a sense of ownership and involvement.

Improving Retention, Loyalty, and Brand Advocacy

Giving customers a say in the brand's processes makes them feel valued and appreciated, enhancing their loyalty. Their direct involvement in product development often leads them to become brand advocates, organically promoting it within their circles.

Examples of Application

A Clothing Brand:

The brand could ask its customers to share their design ideas for an upcoming collection, select the best ones, and acknowledge the contributors in a major marketing campaign.

A Tech Company:

It could create a beta tester community where enthusiasts are given early access to software in exchange for their feedback and suggestions.

A Food Product Company:

It could invite customers to suggest new flavors or variants and then launch the most popular suggestions as limited-edition products, giving credit to the customers who proposed them.

Strategy 7: Predictive Maintenance

IN AN ERA OF SMART devices and IoT, many products can self-monitor and predict when they need maintenance or replacement.

For example, a smart washing machine could alert the owner and the manufacturer when a particular part is nearing its end. This enables the manufacturer to proactively reach out to the customer with solutions, often before the customer realizes there's a problem.

Strategic Overview

The "Predictive Maintenance" strategy capitalizes on the advancements in technology, specifically the Internet of Things (IoT) and Artificial Intelligence (AI). This approach allows brands to proactively address maintenance issues before they become problems, enhancing the overall customer experience and cementing a brand's reputation as a reliable and customer-centric entity.

Key Tasks

Invest in Smart Technology:

Develop or adopt IoT-enabled products that can self-monitor and predict when they may need maintenance or replacement.

Create Responsive Systems:

Develop an after-sales service framework that promptly responds to these smart devices' maintenance alerts.

Proactive Customer Communication:

Create a communication strategy that informs customers of the need for maintenance in a timely and convenient manner.

Recommended Tools

- This strategy primarily utilizes Innovative After-Sales Platforms and Analytics Tools.

- IoT technology forms the backbone of predictive maintenance.

- Analytics tools help predict potential issues and craft suitable responses.

Customer Psychology After-Purchase

Once a purchase is made, customers expect a smooth and trouble-free experience with the product. By predicting maintenance needs and proactively addressing them, brands exceed customer expectations, reinforcing trust and satisfaction.

Improving Retention, Loyalty, and Brand Advocacy

Proactive maintenance reduces the chances of product failure, thereby minimizing customer frustration. This increases retention and strengthens loyalty, as customers appreciate the brand's commitment to maintaining optimal product performance. Customers are likely to share their positive experiences, turning into brand ambassadors.

Examples of Application

A Smart Refrigerator Manufacturer:

The manufacturer could install AI technology to alert both the owner and the company when certain parts require maintenance or replacement, enabling the company to proactively contact the customer with a solution.

A Car Manufacturer:

They could equip their vehicles with sensors to predict potential issues in specific components. On detecting a potential problem, the car's system could notify the manufacturer's service center, which could then contact the customer to schedule a check-up.

A Tech Company Offering IoT Services:

The company could use AI and data analytics to predict and mitigate potential technical issues in their servers or network, ensuring smooth customer service and proactively communicating potential issues.

Strategy 8: AI-Powered Customer Service

LEVERAGE AI CHATBOTS to provide immediate, 24/7 support to customers post-purchase. These bots can answer common queries, guide users through troubleshooting steps, and even schedule appointments with human customer service reps when required.

Strategic Overview

The "AI-Powered Customer Service" strategy leverages artificial intelligence to deliver instant, round-the-clock support to customers post-purchase. The immediacy and availability of this type of support can significantly enhance the customer experience, building a stronger relationship between the brand and its customers.

Key Tasks

Implement AI Chatbots:

Deploy AI chatbots on customer service channels to provide immediate responses to customer queries and to guide customers through troubleshooting steps.

Train the AI:

Regularly update and train the AI chatbots to improve their understanding and to ensure they provide accurate and helpful responses.

Integrate Human Support:

Create a seamless transition between AI support and human customer service representatives for more complex issues.

Recommended Tools

- Primarily, this strategy requires using Innovative After-Sales Platforms, specifically AI chatbot tools.

- Additionally, integrating these chatbots with CRM Systems ensures they have access to customer history and other necessary information to provide personalized support.

Customer Psychology After-Purchase

Post-purchase, customers require quick and accurate solutions to their problems or answers to their queries. AI-powered customer service caters to this immediate need for support, contributing to customer satisfaction and boosting the brand's perceived value.

Improving Retention, Loyalty, and Brand Advocacy

Immediate, effective support post-purchase can significantly enhance customer retention, reducing frustration and ensuring the customer gets the most out of their product. This increases loyalty, and customers will likely recommend a brand that provides exceptional customer service, turning them into brand ambassadors.

Examples of Application

An E-commerce Retailer:

The retailer could use an AI chatbot on their website to immediately address common customer queries regarding returns, shipping, and product details, reducing the load on their human customer service representatives.

A Software Company:

The company could use an AI chatbot to guide users through common troubleshooting steps or to provide guidance on how to use certain features, ensuring users get the most out of their product.

A Telecom Provider:

The provider could use an AI chatbot to help customers with common issues such as balance checks, data plans, or service disruptions, offering immediate support and reducing the need for human intervention.

Strategy 9: Personalized Social Media Engagement

ACTIVELY ENGAGE WITH customers on social media platforms. Respond to their posts, share their content, or even create personalized videos thanking them for their support. This helps create a more personal connection with the brand.

Strategic Overview

The "Personalized Social Media Engagement" strategy seeks to foster a strong customer bond by creating a dynamic, two-way conversation on social media platforms. This approach can humanize your brand and cultivate a more personal and meaningful relationship with customers, enhancing their overall brand experience.

Key Tasks

Social Listening:

Monitor social media platforms for mentions of your brand, product reviews, customer inquiries, or general comments related to your industry.

Engaging with Customers:

Respond to customers' posts, comments, and reviews. This can range from simple acknowledgments or thank you messages to more in-depth interactions.

Sharing User-Generated Content:

Share and spotlight content created by customers, such as unboxing videos, reviews, or posts featuring your products. Always seek permission before sharing user-generated content.

Recommended Tools

- This strategy mainly utilizes Social Media Platforms and CRM Systems.

- Social media platforms will be the primary interaction points.

- CRM systems can be used to track customer interactions and to segment customers for personalized content.

Customer Psychology After-Purchase

After purchasing a product, customers often share their experiences on social media. Engaging with these customers makes them feel seen and valued, demonstrating that the brand is committed to their satisfaction even after the purchase.

Improving Retention, Loyalty, and Brand Advocacy

Positive and personalized engagement with customers on social media can increase customer satisfaction, improving customer retention and loyalty. Furthermore, a customer who has positively interacted with a brand on social media is likelier to become a brand advocate, sharing their positive experiences with their social networks.

Examples of Application

A Cosmetic Brand:

The brand could re-share customer-created makeup tutorials using their products, comment on their posts, and create personalized thank you videos for loyal customers.

A Fitness Equipment Company:

The company could engage with customers who share their fitness journey and achievements using their products, offer tips and encouragement, and feature these customers on their social media platforms.

An Online Retailer:

The retailer could respond to customer reviews and queries on social media, share customer-created unboxing videos or product photos, and create personalized promotional offers for loyal customers.

Strategy 10: Customer Education Webinars

HOLD FREE WEBINARS or live sessions on topics related to your product or industry. This provides ongoing value to customers and positions your brand as a trusted expert.

Strategic Overview

The "Customer Education Webinars" strategy aims to provide customers with continuous value post-purchase by offering free educational content related to your product or industry. By investing in your customers' knowledge, you position your brand as a trusted expert and a valuable resource.

Key Tasks

Topic Identification:

Identify relevant topics that your customers will find interesting and valuable. These topics ideally relate to your product or industry and help customers get more out of your produc

Webinar Creation:

Create engaging, informative webinars. Ensure the content is easy to understand, practical, and directly beneficial to the customers.

Webinar Promotion:

Promote your webinars through various channels like email, social media, and your website to reach as many customers as possible.

Recommended Tools

- For this strategy, Email Marketing and Social Media Platforms are essential tools.

- Email marketing can be used to promote the webinars, while social media can provide an additional promotional channel and a platform for hosting live sessions.

- Webinar software will be required for hosting the sessions.

Customer Psychology After-Purchase

Once customers have made a purchase, they are often eager to learn how to maximize the use of the product. Providing them with additional knowledge and skills enhances their product experience and nurtures a deeper connection with the brand.

Improving Retention, Loyalty, and Brand Advocacy

Customer education webinars increase customer engagement and loyalty by offering continuous value beyond the product itself. Customers who perceive a brand as a trusted advisor are likelier to remain loyal. Furthermore, satisfied customers may share their positive learning experiences with others, acting as brand ambassadors.

Examples of Application

A Gardening Tools Company:

The company could host webinars on different gardening techniques and tips for choosing the right plants based on climate or using their tools most effectively.

A Software Company:

The company could offer free webinars on how to use their software more efficiently, best practices in their industry, or advanced techniques for using their software.

A Health and Wellness Brand:

The brand could host webinars on various health topics, nutrition tips, or exercises that can be done at home. They could also use these sessions to demonstrate the correct use of their products.

Strategy 11: Gamification of Customer Experience

INCENTIVIZE ENGAGEMENT and purchases with gamified elements. This could be as simple as a loyalty points system or as complex as a fully interactive brand app where users can earn rewards.

Strategic Overview

The "Gamification of Customer Experience" strategy enhances customer engagement and retention by incorporating game-like elements into the customer journey.

This could include challenges, points, badges, or rewards to create a fun, interactive post-purchase experience. One innovative method is using personalized "Thank You" eCards to show customers they're valued and appreciated.

Key Tasks

Design a Gamified Customer Journey:

Identify opportunities within your customer interaction points to add elements of gamification. This could be as simple as introducing a point system for customer interaction or as complex as designing an entire gamified customer journey.

Develop Personalized eCards:

Using tools like iGreetu Bespoke, design personalized "Thank You" eCards that can be sent to your customers. These should be tailored to each customer and their purchase, highlighting the value they bring to your business.

Implement and Track:

Roll out the gamified elements and monitor their impact on customer engagement and retention. Adjust and refine as needed based on customer feedback and data.

Recommended Tools

- Innovative After-Sales Platforms such as eCards are critical in the execution of this strategy.

- CRM Systems to track customer interaction and engagement

- Email Marketing Platforms for distribution.

Customer Psychology After-Purchase

Gamification taps into the human desire for achievement and reward. By turning customer interaction into a game, customers are more likely to engage consistently with your brand, which can lead to improved retention and brand loyalty.

Improving Retention, Loyalty, and Brand Advocacy

By maBy making the post-purchase experience more engaging and enjoyable, customers are likelier to stick with your brand and develop loyalty. The personal touch of a "Thank You" eCard can foster feelings of appreciation and satisfaction, which can help transform customers into brand advocates.

Examples of Application

An Online Retailer:

Offers points for customer actions like writing reviews, sharing on social media, or referring friends. These points can be redeemed for discounts or exclusive perks. They also send personalized "Thank You" eCards after every purchase, with a unique discount code for the next one.

A Sightseeing Bus Operator:

Engages with customers post-tour by offering a free range of eCards featuring stunning views and landmarks of the city they visited. This serves as a memento of the experience and encourages customers to share these eCards with their friends and family, increasing brand exposure.

A Fast Food Chain:

Uses personalized eCards to provide digital coupons for the next purchase. These eCards could be designed with enticing images of their menu items. They could be easily shared with friends, driving repeat business and attracting new customers through word-of-mouth referrals.

Strategy 12: Proactive Feedback Collection

BE SURE TO COME TO you with feedback before customers come to you. Instead, use email or in-app surveys to seek out their thoughts and feelings about your product proactively. Not only does this show you value their opinion, but it also provides you with valuable data for future improvements.

Strategic Overview

The "Proactive Feedback Collection" strategy emphasizes the importance of actively seeking customer input rather than waiting for it to be voluntarily provided. This approach demonstrates that you value your customers' experiences and insights and provides valuable data to help improve your product and customer service.

Key Tasks

Design Surveys:

Craft concise, easy-to-understand surveys that encourage customers to share their thoughts and experiences. The questions should cover their experiences with the product, service, and overall brand interaction.

Distribute Surveys:

Leverage Email Marketing Platforms or in-app messaging systems to distribute these surveys to your customers. The timing of sending these surveys should be thoughtfully considered to optimize response rates.

Analyze Feedback:

Collect and analyze the feedback received. Look for trends, common issues, or areas of praise that can help shape your business strategy moving forward.

Recommended Tools

- Feedback and Survey Tools, Email Marketing Platforms, and CRM Systems are vital for this strategy.

- Email marketing platforms and in-app messaging tools can be used to distribute surveys.

- CRM systems can store and manage the collected data for analysis.

Customer Psychology After-Purchase

After making a purchase, customers appreciate brands that continue to show interest in their experience and satisfaction. Asking for their opinion indicates that their voice matters, fostering a sense of value and connection.

Improving Retention, Loyalty, and Brand Advocacy

Proactively seeking feedback improves your product and demonstrates to customers that their opinions are valued, contributing to greater customer satisfaction and loyalty. Happy customers who feel heard and appreciated are likelier to become brand advocates, sharing their positive experiences with others.

Examples of Application

A Tech Gadgets Company:

THE ART OF AFTER-SALES MARKETING

After a month of the purchase, the company sends out a survey asking about the customer's experience with the gadget, its features, any issues faced, and any suggestions they have for improvement.

An E-commerce Retailer:

Regularly sends out surveys post-purchase, asking about customers' experiences with the shopping process, delivery, and product quality.

A Health and Fitness App:

Uses in-app surveys to collect user feedback on features, workout plans, user interface, and other elements that can be improved.

Each of these strategies, whether it's continuing the customer journey with your brand or leveraging AI for customer service, contributes uniquely to the multifaceted realm of after-sales marketing.

We've witnessed how customers can be engaged, appreciated, and inspired post-purchase. We've seen how personalization can spark delight, co-creation can foster deeper connections, and proactive feedback collection can underline the customer's value to the company.

These strategies aim to do more than just resolve problems or retain customers. They are crafted to paint a vibrant picture of an immersive, enriching, and continual relationship between the brand and the customer.

As we conclude this exploration, we leave you with this palette of strategies you can adapt, combine, and tailor to your brand's unique needs and aspirations.

Chapter 6: The Future of After-Sales Marketing

THE DYNAMIC LANDSCAPE of after-sales marketing is forever changing and evolving. Just as the customer journey has grown beyond the point of purchase, so has the world of after-sales marketing grown beyond mere customer service.

A keen eye on the horizon reveals emerging trends that hold the potential to revolutionize the way businesses interact with their customers post-purchase. Companies must anticipate these changes and evolve with these trends to create experiences that continue to delight and retain customers.

Increasing Personalization and Customization:

As consumers expect more personalized experiences, businesses must invest further in data analytics and AI to tailor after-sales interactions to individual customer preferences and behaviors.

Rise of AI and Chatbots:

The usage of AI-driven customer interaction tools, such as chatbots and virtual assistants, will continue to grow. As these technologies become more sophisticated, they will be able to provide more personalized and human-like interactions, providing instant support and leaving humans free to handle more complex issues.

Integration of IoT in After-Sales Service:

Internet of Things (IoT) technology can enable businesses to monitor product usage and provide proactive service – for instance, predictive maintenance or replenishment of supplies. This trend toward "servitization" can help companies build stronger customer relationships and increase customer loyalty.

Expansion of Omnichannel After-Sales Support:

The line between different sales and support channels will continue to blur as businesses aim to provide seamless after-sales support across multiple channels. Customers expect to be able to interact with companies via their preferred channel, whether that's email, social media, live chat, phone, or in-person.

Increased Use of AR:

Augmented Reality (AR) technology holds exciting potential for after-sales marketing. For instance, businesses could use AR to provide more immersive product demonstrations or virtual customer support.

More Co-Creation Opportunities:

Businesses will involve customers more in the creation and development process. This includes product development and co-creation of content, such as user-generated reviews, photos, and videos.

Greater Emphasis on Sustainability:

As consumers become more conscious about sustainability, businesses will need to consider how their after-sales practices can reflect this. This could involve steps like using eco-friendly packaging for product returns, providing repair services to extend the life of products, or setting up product take-back schemes for recycling.

Opinion: Sustainable choices are not immune to the pressures of a global economic climate.

The role of sustainability in the future of after-sales marketing cannot be understated, but recent trends show a more complex picture that challenges the assumed trajectory.

A study by GWI, The Future of Retail: 10 Retail Trends for 2023[1], offers some fascinating insights into this evolving landscape. Although it is reassuring that 57% of consumers are willing to pay more for eco-friendly products, a deeper dive into the data uncovers some unsettling trends.

The desire to make more sustainable choices, it appears, is not immune to the pressures of a global economic climate. Over the past two years, consumers prioritizing eco-friendly products have dipped by 8%.

This downward trend has been particularly pronounced among low-income earners, with the number prioritizing eco-friendly brands decreasing by 11% since Q3 2020.

1. https://blog.gwi.com/marketing/retail-trends/

The future of after-sales marketing holds exciting opportunities for businesses to deepen their relationships with customers. Brands anticipating these trends and adapting accordingly will be better positioned to create lasting impressions and cultivate customer loyalty.

Therefore, the masterpiece of after-sales marketing continues to be a work in progress, continually adding new layers of depth and color to the canvas of customer experience.

Conclusion: Becoming the Master Artist

AS WE CLOSE THE PAGES of this explorative journey into the vibrant and transformative world of after-sales marketing, we must acknowledge the powerful impact this practice has in sculpting enduring relationships with customers, fostering brand loyalty, and amplifying brand awareness.

After-sales marketing, we realize, is not merely a business necessity but an artistic opportunity to create memorable experiences and lasting impressions that resonate deeply with our customers.

Throughout our exploration, we've seen that the greatest after-sales artists view every customer interaction as a brushstroke on the canvas of their brand narrative.

They understand that each touchpoint and experience contributes to the overall picture. They leverage the full spectrum of their marketing palette, utilizing tools from social media and CRM systems to innovative platforms.

These artists do not simply respond to customer issues; they proactively shape the post-purchase experience, guiding customers along a journey that deepens their connection with the brand. They design compelling after-sales narratives that tell a story where the customer is the protagonist, and the brand is a supportive ally, helping them achieve their goals and aspirations.

Moreover, these master artists recognize that their work is never finished. They understand that the art of after-sales is an ongoing process of creation, refinement, and evolution. They embrace a mindset of continuous learning and improvement, adapt to the changing colors of customer expectations and market dynamics, and constantly seek new ways to enhance their after-sales artistry.

As we step away from this book, let us embrace the artist's role in our marketing endeavors. Let us harness the power of after-sales marketing to paint our masterpieces, creating a vibrant gallery of customer experiences that delight our customers and impact the world.

Remember, the canvas is in your hands, the palette is at your disposal, and the potential to create something truly remarkable is immense. So, unleash your creativity, and become the master artist of your brand's after-sales journey. The gallery of unforgettable customer experiences awaits your masterpiece.

Epilogue: The Meaning of the Tale

REFLECTING ON OUR JOURNEY through the world of after-sales marketing, we can liken it to the story of the Zen master artist and the emperor. Like the artist, we have immersed ourselves in the landscape of our customer's experiences, taking the time to understand and become a part of their journey.

The artist's painted path is a metaphor for after-sales marketing - a trail that intrigues the customer, inviting them to embark on a new journey beyond their initial purchase. When we provide customers with an engaging, personalized experience, we're not just selling a product or service but a path - an opportunity for them to deepen their relationship with our brand.

Just as the artist and the emperor walked down the painted path and never returned, so too does an effective after-sales strategy guide the customer on a continuing journey with our brand. It takes them deeper into the brand experience, strengthening their connection and loyalty and ensuring they continue to choose us for their future needs.

Like the emperor, our customers may become so engaged with the experience we provide that they don't feel the need to return to the marketplace, choosing instead to stay with a brand that understands and values them. Thus, our journey in after-sales marketing, like the artist's painted path, leads us to unending possibilities and opportunities.

About the Author

VLADISLAV DOBROKHOTOV is a seasoned professional, highly acclaimed in Marketing and Customer Relations. A Liveryman of the Worshipful Company of Marketors, Vladislav's work embodies a deep understanding of market dynamics and customer retention strategies, critical components of the field.

Currently serving as the Executive Director of The British & Commonwealth Chamber of Commerce in Finland, Vladislav excels in creating personalized experiences for his members. His unique approach, emphasizing emotional engagement, contributes to high member satisfaction and loyalty. In this role, Vladislav's work transcends traditional business boundaries, significantly impacting the international business community.

Vladislav is also the founder of igreetu, an innovative digital eCard platform. This platform revolutionizes the after-sales process by providing an additional avenue for businesses to express gratitude, appreciate customer loyalty, and enhance brand image. With igreetu, Vladislav combines his understanding of customer psychology with technological innovation, offering an unmatched tool for businesses to enrich their customer relationships post-purchase.

A champion of creating and nurturing lasting customer relationships, Vladislav's work is a testament to his commitment to after-sales marketing. His endeavors as an executive and an entrepreneur offer valuable insights for anyone looking to master the art of customer retention and loyalty.

References

1. Harward Business Review, "The Value of Keeping the Right Customers" by Amy Gallo
   https://hbr.org/2014/10/the-value-of-keeping-the-right-customers
2. Bain & Company, "Prescription for Cutting Costs" By Fred Reichheld
   https://media.bain.com/Images/BB_Prescription_cutting_costs.pdf
3. Nielsen, "Consumer Trust in Online, Social and Mobile Advertising Grows"
   https://www.nielsen.com/insights/2012/consumer-trust-in-online-social-and-mobile-advertising-grows/
4. Nielsen, "5 brand building factors for emerging media"
   https://www.nielsen.com/insights/2023/brand-building-factors-for-emerging-media/
5. Salesforce, "Personalization, Data Security, and Speed Drive Customer Loyalty Amid Uncertainty"
   https://www.salesforce.com/news/stories/customer-spending/
6. Salesforce, "What Are Customer Expectations, and How Have They Changed?"
   https://www.salesforce.com/resources/articles/customer-expectations/
7. McKinsey & Company, "Prediction: The future of CX" by Rachel Diebner, David Malfara, Kevin Neher, Mike Thompson, and Maxence Vancauwenberghe
   https://www.mckinsey.com/capabilities/growth-marketing-and-sales/our-insights/prediction-the-future-of-cx

8. Nucleus Research, "CRM Pays Back $8.71 for Every Dollar Spent" https://nucleusresearch.com/wp-content/uploads/2018/05/o128-CRM-pays-back-8.71-for-every-dollar-spent.pdf

9. SuperOffice, "3 Effective Ways to Measure Customer Satisfaction" https://www.superoffice.com/blog/measure-customer-satisfaction/

10. Adobe, "If You Think Email Is Dead, Think Again" https://business.adobe.com/blog/perspectives/if-you-think-email-is-dead-think-again

11. Omnisend, "2020 Ecommerce Statistics Report" https://www.omnisend.com/resources/reports/ecommerce-statistics-report-2021/

12. Campaign Monitor, "The New Rules of Email Marketing" https://www.campaignmonitor.com/resources/guides/email-marketing-new-rules/

13. Microsoft, "State of Global Customer Service Report" https://info.microsoft.com/ww-landing-global-state-of-customer-service.html

14. Wonderflow, "How to utilize Customer Feedback in Product Development" https://www.wonderflow.ai/blog/customer-feedback-with-product-development/

15. BrightLocal, "Local Consumer Review Survey" https://www.brightlocal.com/research/local-consumer-review-survey/#[1]

16. Apptentive, "2020 Mobile Customer Engagement Benchmark Report" https://mobile.alchemer.com/2020-mobile-customer-engagement-benchmark-report

---

1. https://www.brightlocal.com/research/local-consumer-review-survey/

17. Pew Research Center, "Social Media Fact Sheet"
    https://www.pewresearch.org/internet/fact-sheet/social-media/

18. GlobalWebIndex, "Social Media Trends 2020"
    https://www.gwi.com/reports/social-2020

19. Sprout Social, "Index™ 2020: Above and Beyond"
    https://media.sproutsocial.com/uploads/2020-Sprout-Social-Index-Above-and-Beyond.pdf

20. Yotpo, "The State of Brand Loyalty 2022"
    https://www.yotpo.com/the-state-of-brand-loyalty-2022/emotional-loyalty-is-in-and-has-to-be-earned/

21. Bond Brand Loyalty, "The Loyalty Report 2016"
    https://info.bondbrandloyalty.com/the-2016-bond-loyalty-report-press-release-us

22. Bond Brand Loyalty, "The Loyalty Report 2020"
    https://info.bondbrandloyalty.com/tlr-2020

23. MicroStrategy, "2020 Global State of Enterprise Analytics"
    https://www3.microstrategy.com/getmedia/db67a6c7-0bc5-41fa-82a9-bb14ec6868d6/2020-Global-State-of-Enterprise-Analytics.pdf

24. Nucleus Research, "Analytics pays back $13.01 for every dollar spent"
    https://nucleusresearch.com/research/single/analytics-pays-back-13-01-for-every-dollar-spent/